I0759780

Advance Praise for *The Rehab Playbook*

"Jaime Vinck's depth and scope of experience makes her the perfect person to write a book demystifying addiction treatment. Her style of writing immediately invites the reader in as she offers a vivid description of what to ask and expect as one reaches out for help. Understanding the many fears, doubts, and hopelessness experienced, she knows the power of good treatment. It can be frightening to let go of one's addiction and put faith in a process that most have only seen portrayed via the media culture and hearsay. *The Rehab Playbook* quickly empowers the often skeptical and scared reader to gain confidence in their decision to live life differently, realizing they can enter treatment, stay in treatment, and embrace a recovery process."

—**Claudia Black**, PhD, addiction and trauma specialist, author of *Undaunted Hope: Stories of Healing from Trauma, Depression and Addictions*

THE REHAB PLAYBOOK

THE REHAB PLAYBOOK

Demystifying Addiction Treatment

JAIME WELSH VINCK, MC, LPC

A REGALO PRESS BOOK
ISBN: 979-8-88845-633-0
ISBN (eBook): 979-8-88845-634-7

Cover Design by Jim Villaflores

Publishing Team:
Founder and Publisher – Gretchen Young
Editorial Assistant – Caitlyn Limbaugh
Managing Editor – Aleigha Koss
Production Manager – Kate Harris
Production Editor – Rachel Paul

This book, as well as any other Regalo Press publications, may be purchased in bulk quantities at a special discounted rate. Contact orders@regalopress.com for more information.

As part of the mission of Regalo Press, a donation is being made to the Addiction Research Institute, as chosen by the author. Find out more about this organization at www.addictionresearchinstitute.org.

This is a work of nonfiction. All people, locations, events, and situations are portrayed to the best of the author's memory.

Regalo Press
New York • Nashville
regalopress.com

Published in the United States of America
1 2 3 4 5 6 7 8 9 10

In honor of everyone who has ever been brave enough to walk through the doors of a treatment center, to heal, to work, or to visit.

In honor of my husband, Bill, who has always seen a light in me that had never been more than a flickering flame.

In honor of my parents, Joseph and Jean. Although we said goodbye too soon, you are my constant inspiration to live a meaningful life for us all.

For my children Patrick, Joseph, and Alexandra, I am so grateful for the gift of being your mom.

For my grandchildren Vera, Nora, and Beckham, I promise to never stop trying to make the world a better place for you.

CONTENTS

INTRODUCTION

HOW A PLAYBOOK CHANGES THE WAY WE VIEW—AND DO—REHAB

"Let us agree that we shall never forget one another, and whatever happens, remember how good it felt when we were all here together, united by a good and decent feeling which made us better people, better probably than we would otherwise have been."

—FYODOR DOSTOYEVSKY

You've come to this book because you or someone you care about is playing a very dangerous game with an invisible opponent—addiction. In a game, or even a battle, there is a winner and a loser—and you are here because one thing is certain: addiction *cannot* win.

Like so many professionals on the front lines in the treatment and recovery industry, I have witnessed what happens when the game or battle is won by our evil opponent. As I was growing up, alcohol was the villain in my family story. I grew up in a family plagued by trauma, loss, grief, depression, and of course, alcohol. My cousin and I still joke that we were raised in the basement of a funeral home. The loss of each loved one—and the drinking that came after—took its toll on us. There were fewer family gatherings, no family trips, and when there were, arguments broke out. There were alcohol-related fatal and near fatal car crashes, arrests, and involuntary commitments to a psych ward. No matter what happened; however, my sober father held everyone together, until he passed away at age forty-three from lung cancer. Losing my father and the steadiness he provided at just thirteen years old shattered my heart and my extended family into a million pieces. Why am I sharing this with you? Because, like so many other recovery professionals, my experiences shaped my decision to go into the addiction treatment field, which gave me the opportunity to help families like mine. Being a part of others' healing journeys and helping them navigate the darkest days of their lives put my heart and soul back together.

As a clinician, CEO, president, and thought leader in the treatment industry for more than twenty years, I have met thousands of patients and families like yours who have made the difficult and heroic decision to ask for help. I have been on the front lines of treatment as both a primary and family therapist, working with families and clients before, during, and after treatment. Throughout my decades of practice, there have been many changes and improvements in addiction treatment. We have expanded both access and the quality of care that is available. Many fine treatment programs have opened at all levels of care, as well as the introduction to medication-assisted treatment, to meet the demand for services. However, two things have remained constant. One, by the time the patients and families get to us, their lives are in shambles. They often face dire consequences (such as jail, divorce, unemployment, or financial ruin) if they don't get help. Two, the treatment process terrifies them.

Addiction is at a record high, despite advances in our understanding and treatment of the invisible opponent. According to the Substance Abuse and Mental Health Services Administration, or SAMHSA, in 2020, one hundred thousand fatal overdoses were recorded in the United States, which is the highest number ever recorded. Additionally in 2020, the Center for Disease Control or CDC reported that more than 13 percent of Americans—or forty-three million people—said they began or substantially increased their substance use as a coping mechanism during the pandemic. But all is not lost. With this increase in usage, there is increased awareness of addiction and in creative options for reaching out for help. Proof of this is the explosion of virtual therapy platforms such as BetterHelp, Talkspace, and Cerebral since the onset of COVID-19. This is fantastic; however, reaching out for help and getting treatment are two different things. According to the American Society of Addiction Medicine, only one out of every ten people who have addictions get treatment.

Why are treatment and recovery elusive for so many? Some reasons are more obvious, like limited financial resources, lack of understanding of insurance benefits, and the stigma associated with addiction and cultural implications. Another reason is more insidious—fear: fear of the unknown, fear of facing one's inner demons, and fear of the treatment process itself.

Although treatment centers have been in existence since the 1930s, the therapeutic process remains shrouded in mystery. We see billboards, TV commercials, social media ads, and so forth showing beautiful facilities and happy looking people. None of it seems real or attainable. Even if you or a loved one has been in treatment before, the idea of starting all over again can be daunting and stop you in your tracks. You may even wonder… *what's going to be different this time?* You may not feel prepared to make what just might be the most important decision in your life—to go against the opponent armed with information, a strategy, and a positive mindset to emerge the winner.

Not to worry. I'm here to cheer you on and offer you information. I believe in the transformational force of love, community, and commitment to something greater than ourselves. Early in my career, I saw the power of support within a community of treatment professionals who are committed to "coach" you throughout your recovery journey. Equally as important, I witnessed the invaluable transformational influence fellow recovery seekers have with each other, acting as "teammates" against an opponent they all want to defeat. This book serves as your playbook, your support, and your community all in one.

When patients or their families pick up that one-thousand-pound phone, well-intentioned rehab centers assure them that they are making the right decision in seeking care and remind them that their future depends on the successful completion of treatment. Reluctantly, the patients put their lives in the hands of the stranger on the phone—the stranger who asked them to take a leap of faith and to trust the process, long before having earned the right to do so. Often, the potential patient will hang up the phone and talk themselves out of going to treatment.

Who can blame them? There is too much to know and not enough information and context to go around. Would we throw someone in a boxing ring who never even learned the art of a left hook? Or would we expect to fight a war on a battlefield where we have never stepped foot? Being unprepared or even in the dark about a world we must visit despite not speaking the language can make us feel even more hopeless and confused than when we first picked up the phone.

For too many people, that hopelessness causes them to retreat on the field and let the addiction win. This is why I created a playbook, a tactical guide, that demystifies rehabilitation, organizes one's thoughts and concerns so they can be managed, and not only shows that healing is possible but also outlines the "plays" to use to make it possible. "Healing is Possible" and "Expect a Miracle" have both been taglines for treatment centers where I have worked. This is not just marketing hype. Healing *is* possible; I've seen it firsthand with thousands of people who have experienced the miracle of lasting recovery. There is hope. I know this is true because I have the privilege of being surrounded by hope every day.

Throughout my career, I have been humbled by the experience of participating in someone's sacred recovery journey. Patients come to us on their knees, their lives in shambles and relationships shattered, and often after an overdose, arrest, or suicide attempt. Entering someone's sacred space without judgment and staying with them in what can feel like a burning building is one of the greatest gifts of my life. I have heard clinicians tell their patients, "I'm going to love you till you love yourself." We become their lifeline.

Using my decades' worth of experience, research, and first-line position on the playing field of treatment and rehabilitation, I have written *The Rehab Playbook* to provide you with the steps, tools, and yes, the winning plays, so you can strategize the fight against the most difficult opponent of your life—addiction. You will learn how to get the most from your "coaches," along with stories of the power of your community and your teammates unified against a common enemy.

What Is Rehabilitation for Addiction?

The process of assisting people to recover from substance use disorders or other behavioral addictions is the definition of rehabilitation. The goals are threefold: help people sustain abstinence from their addiction, improve physical health and tend to mental health, and acquire skills and strategies to achieve long-term recovery maintenance. There are many forms of addiction rehabilitation. They are determined by a person's particular needs, priorities, proclivities, and degree of their addiction. We will discuss the forms and options based on these characteristics in chapter 7.

How to Use This Book

In the business world, a playbook is an organized set of processes, best practices, and strategies. Often, the business playbook will define roles for the team members involved with the shared goal of growth and success (a.k.a. making a profit). In a sports setting, playbooks are constructed and implemented for the win. It clearly spells out the rules and the creative offensive and defensive plays, which often involve the collaboration of one or more willing teammates.

When using a playbook in the context of addiction treatment, the stakes are much higher, as we are dealing with people's lives. But the necessity for understanding options, spelling out best practices, and singling out the realities of the playing field is clear. What does winning in rehab look like? What do growth and success resemble? While this playbook isn't about the craftiest way to score a goal or conduct a company-wide conference, like a sports or business playbook, *The Rehab Playbook* is about clearly and concisely offering a shot—your shot—at a reasonable quality of life and the restoration of relationships. It is my hope that this book will help you see the shot and have the confidence to take it.

In treatment, the best plans are highly individualized, encouraging plenty of client input. *The Rehab Playbook* is no different. The processes and best practices will be the pillars on which to depend during times of high stress. These plays are non-emotional, practical, and solution focused, rooted in my real-world experiences that I have seen make or break someone's treatment. These are things that come up over and over again and become game changers in someone's experience.

The Rehab Playbook provides useful information by providing the steps, tools, and knowledge necessary to increase the odds of a positive experience. The information is organized to provide a deeper understanding of the treatment process: from making the decision on when and where to seek treatment, to navigating the process financially, to setting reasonable expectations on daily activities, duration, and family involvement. In these pages, you will find specific questions to ask, along with what to look for and what to avoid when exploring various treatment centers. When you or your loved one agrees to get care, it is essential to find the program that is the best fit. There may only be one shot, and we must do everything possible to get it right.

The structure of this playbook is designed to be reliable and easy to navigate. All sections will empower you to make the playbook your own by taking the steps and completing the tasks in each play. These steps will guide you before, during, and after treatment. Regardless of where you are in your treatment journey, there will be a section that will speak to and benefit you.

In treatment and recovery, we practice "meeting someone where they are at." *The Rehab Playbook* mirrors this philosophy. While in a time of stress and fear, sitting down and reading a full book may not be an option. Getting an answer, moving on, and then returning to the playbook is a consistent alternative with its structure and intent. Start with the play that resonates and master the steps to take. "Where you will be at" in preparing for treatment for yourself or a loved one will vary from day-to-day. Honor your choice, go to that section, and get to work. You don't have to read the chapter in its entirety in order to get something out of the playbook. The highly designed features make it possible to gather information at a glance.

The Rehab Playbook will also mitigate some of the fear and stigma that holds people back from seeking treatment by introducing interviews with industry professionals that are raw and revealing, as well as encouraging and reassuring. You'll hear directly from these meetings in chapter breaks called "Team Meeting." Team meetings are an integral part of the treatment experience, and these featured interviews will provide insights not previously available outside the walls of a treatment center. These interviews, which I conducted exclusively for this book, provide a view from those who work, or have worked, in treatment centers. Most have been through treatment themselves.

Their words are capable of inspiring those struggling in silence to begin their healing journey. If you are looking for a treatment center for yourself or a loved one, you will be relieved and reassured to discover how much of these individuals' hearts and souls go into their work. There are good guys and bad guys in every profession, and in every treatment center. Thankfully, there are far more heroes than villains, and two of the goals of this book is to introduce some true heroes and recognize the incredible work going on in the behavioral health space.

Throughout the book, the importance of sharing in group settings and establishing community among fellow recovery seekers will be showcased. I recount special connections forged in group therapy settings, where addicts become teammates united to fight against a shared opponent. These features are titled "Circle of Support."

Finally, because many of you are family members or friends of someone suffering with substance use disorder, you will find a section called "For Fans and Family" that speaks directly to your needs and challenges. If you are struggling with your addiction and considering treatment yourself, reading these sections will offer some clarity on what your loved ones are feeling and thinking. In each chapter, this section bridges the gap between you and those you care about. By working with the facts, not assumptions, we can reduce the shame that prevents people from trusting and speaking openly. This shared knowledge can help bring you together to increase success and build an even stronger relationship.

Practical Tools While Reading

As you work through the plays in each section, your *why* for picking up *The Rehab Playbook* in the first place may change. You will experience emotional ups and downs or feel resentful or completely overwhelmed by emotions. That is to be expected. In each section, you will be prompted by a section called "Work It." Here, you can curate and use practical tools, such as affirmations, creating a mantra (my mantra is "All is Well"), and introspective exercises, all of which we utilize in treatment. This experience is uniquely yours, and you will be supported and reminded to practice self-care each step of the way. When we make something our own, we internalize the experience and learning. Throughout our playbook, as your coach, I will often encourage working a 12-step programs. The twelve steps are a set of guiding principles in addiction treatment that outline a course of action for confronting challenges related to alcohol, drug, and compulsive behaviors. The 12-step program and other support groups will be discussed in detail later in our playbook. As you prepare to run on to the field, I will borrow a 12-step common phrase: "It works if you work it." I strongly suggest being prepared to use all your tools while reading and working the plays. As your confidence grows, hope and courage will replace darkness and fear.

CHAPTER 1

JOINING THE TEAM

The Plays for Making the Biggest Decision of Your Life

"Not everything that is faced can be changed; but nothing can be changed until it is faced."

—JAMES BALDWIN

A mother watched her daughter trying to move a heavy rock. The longer it took, the more frustrated the daughter became. No matter what the girl tried, the rock would not budge.

The mother asked, "Are you using all of your strength?"

"Yes, mom," the girl cried, "I promise I am."

The mother looked at her daughter and said, "No, you are not using all of your strength." The girl did not understand and cried even harder.

"I am right here, and you did not ask for my help," the mother explained. "Together, we could have moved the rock."

This story is reminiscent of what happens when someone is struggling with the rock of addiction. They truly believe that they are doing everything that they can to cut down, hide it, or quit on their own—other than reach out to someone for help, that is. Perhaps it is you who is carrying a bag of rocks that represents the pain, suffering, and traumas of our lives. Maybe you have come to find this book because of the following:

- Your drinking is out of control, and there have been consequences (loss of relationships, legal troubles, work issues, and so on), and you are afraid and embarrassed.
- Your loved one's behavior is worrisome (for instance, too much drinking or drugging). You know they need help, but you just don't know your options or how to approach them.
- Your coworker smells like alcohol and is going through a rough time. You are sympathetic, but enough already.
- You know that you need help; however, you are afraid that "rehab" is only for the rich and famous. You wonder what options there are for "normal" people.
- You know plenty of people who went to "rehab" and started drinking/drugging right after they got home. You question if treatment ever works.
- You went to rehab and relapsed. You wonder if you can get another chance.
- You need help but you can't step out of your life for thirty days due to family and work commitments.
- You are terrified by fentanyl and the risk of overdose.
- You don't buy into the 12-step process because you don't have a higher power, and, to you, it feels like a cult.

- You are a healthcare professional and many of your patients seem to be struggling with addiction.
- Your loved one, coworker, or friend gave you this book. You are angry and hurt, yet something is telling you to give it a glance.
- You wonder what kind of people work in rehabs.
- You have been to rehab and wonder what it would be like to work in a treatment center.

Whatever your reasons or how heavy your bag of rocks may be, seeking treatment is the willingness to set down that bag and unpack the rocks one at a time. Treatment is about trusting someone enough to carry your bag of rocks and allowing yourself to feel the relief of not carrying the burdens. Or realizing that if we set our rocks down, we won't float away without them. In fact, we find that we might feel good.

If this book is to be our official playbook, how do we decide that we are ready for the team—a proverbial one and a literal one, in which we become members united with our intentions and the intentions of others to engage in the fight of a lifetime? There are a number of plays we can practice to get us to a place where giving and receiving help feels more natural. Right now, shame, confusion, regret, and fear may make joining a team in recovery feel uncomfortable and foreign—especially when we are not proud of our actions or where we are in our lives. But asking for help as well as giving it is part of being human and a member of society. We are literally hardwired for it, although we rarely remember that.

Research conducted by Stanford University's Dr. Xuan Zhao shows that people hesitate to ask for help because they inaccurately assume that other people are more interested in themselves. However, what Dr. Zhao discovered was the opposite. Other people are often happy to help, with some reporting relief that someone who needs help reached out. She also concluded that people who have been braving it alone were not fooling anyone. In other words, we are not nearly as good as we think when it comes to hiding our need for support.

Play 1. Defend Yourself from Your Defenses

Making the decision to rehabilitate yourself is riddled with complexities. Maybe the decision seems simple…too simple. Or you feel ambushed by loved ones and a little coerced and judged. Or perhaps you feel that going into treatment is a bit drastic. These are all normal responses because they are rooted in a self-protection tool called a "defense mechanism." Our first play is to understand how our defense mechanisms prevent us from—or stall—getting started in rehab. Denial is one of our biggest defense mechanisms and is typically ubiquitous in substance use disorder. Denial is an opponent within the opponent of addiction. Breaking through our denial will lead us to an open field, where our options become clearer and can take us closer to our goals.

Simply put, denial is when we do not accept reality. Our brain creates denial to protect us from what we cannot face. Why actively choose to feel emotional anguish when we can turn away from it, pretending it never happened? Whether it's the experience of loss, guilt, shame, or any other emotional burden, denial is how our brain refuses to experience it. By their nature, defense mechanisms aren't necessarily bad, as they can allow us to get through painful experiences. But they become problematic when they are our "go-to" coping strategy and keep us detached from our reality. Denial is the defense mechanism most commonly described in substance use disorder; however, rationalization and justification play a role as well.

When someone with an addiction is in denial, their mind creates a system of rationalizations, justifying their harmful behaviors. Rationalization and justification are extensions of denial, as well as defense mechanisms, that help us avoid the hard things like admitting we need help, we hurt someone we love, or we screwed up at work. Rationalization is an attempt to provide logical reasons for unacceptable behaviors. For example, a client once told me that her words were slurred and incoherent in her voicemail message because she had dental work done. Another explained that he had to "get loaded" because he was under so much stress at work, or if I knew how horrible their mother was, I would understand why he needed to use.

The human mind has an extraordinary ability to come up with reasons to make us feel better about our behavior. It is often said that when someone is in their active addiction, they lie when the truth would be just fine, or when their lips are moving, they are lying. These lies are a part of denial. They are often lying to themselves and believing it. This type of lying is particularly dangerous, as it justifies our unhealthy and hurtful actions.

Work It!

When I was a therapist in residential treatment, I asked my clients to carry a pen and paper with them and jot down every time that they told a lie. Try it yourself. Big or small, you'll be illuminated by having tangible evidence of how ingrained lies may have become in your communication style.

1. Ask yourself: Can you explain why you told a lie, when the truth would've been fine?
2. Consider whether you have lost credibility with loved ones who can't trust anything, big or small, that you say. (More on this in the family communication section.)
3. Ask yourself: Why would the truth have been so hard to say out loud?

Other Ways We Experience Denial

There are many other types of denial that are important when considering when and how to ask for help. Each of the following are types of defense mechanisms that keep us trapped in a state of denial regarding the nature of addiction.

- Minimization
- Avoidance
- Control

- Normalizing
- Blaming others

Minimization

Minimization happens when you downplay the impact that your behaviors have had on your lives and the lives of others. Statements might include the following:

- I drink less than others whose lives aren't a mess, so it's not like I have a problem.
- I'm make more money than most people.
- I still have a job.
- I don't use every day.
- I'm not hurting anyone—my partner and kids still have a great life.

Avoidance

Avoidance is dodging or escaping distressful thoughts or emotions rather than dealing with them. Substance use itself could assist in avoidance if we turn to a substance as a coping mechanism that keeps us out of our emotions. Many folks use substances to cope with depression, anxiety, or anger, realizing through treatment that they were living in fear of their emotions and preferring the numbness associated with substance use. Some examples can include the following:

- I drink to quiet my mind.
- I'm more relaxed.
- It makes me better socially.

- All my friends only like me when I'm half in the bag and having fun.
- I have a high level of stress in my life.

Some people want to avoid boredom or loneliness. Avoiding boredom is a common justification for continued drinking and drugging. Some examples include the following:

- There's nothing else to do.
- This is the only thing going on in this city.
- There's not a lot of places to go for people my age.
- I can't have fun when I'm sober.

In early recovery, confronting perceived boredom is an important step. It involves reframing the idea that boredom is really about the fact that your identity has been taken over by drug- or alcohol-related activities, as well as "friends" that have the same priorities. Many folks in early recovery will tell us that they don't know what they enjoy doing, and a great deal of time is spent reattaching to parts of ourselves and loved ones that have been overshadowed by addiction. Addiction is a very jealous companion and leaves very little room for anything or anyone else.

Control

In order to make ourselves feel better and deny the seriousness of our situations, we sometimes talk ourselves into believing we are in control. Believing we are in control of our opponent gives us a false sense of security, which is very dangerous, especially when using. The fallacy of control makes us overestimate or underestimate the level of control we have over a situation, thereby leading us to let our guard down and use more.

Do any of these phrases about overestimating one's control sound familiar?

- I can stop whenever I want.
- I can do it on my own.
- If I really thought I had a problem, I could quit.
- I've got this under control.

How about these phrases about underestimating one's control?

- I'm at the point of no return.
- It's a disease, so I'm powerless to do anything about it.
- My father was an addict, my grandfather was an addict, so it is genetic.
- It's not my fault…my parents made me this way.

Normalizing

For someone struggling with an addiction, normalizing is a way to diminish a sense of personal responsibility and focus on the entertainment value of a behavior rather than the harm. Common statements may include the following:

- Everyone's doing it.
- It's normal.
- Who doesn't drink!
- You drink more than I do.
- If alcohol was really bad, it would be illegal.
- It's natural.
- It's prescribed.

- It's a special event.
- I'm over eighteen.
- It's Friday.
- It's a social thing.

Blaming Others

This consists of not taking responsibility and blaming others for what is going wrong. Blaming sometimes prevents people from asking for help, especially if they have had a negative experience in treatment. Statements might include the following:

- If you spent more time with me, I wouldn't have to run to the bar/casino.
- I drink because of all the pressure you put on me.

I am not suggesting that every person with a substance use disorder is in denial. People with substance use disorder and their loved ones are, however, in various stages of contemplating change, and that denial and the related coping mechanisms can become a roadblock to change and recovery.

Play 2. Ask for Help

One of my clients, who we will call Susanne, was a social drinker (wine with dinner, parties, holidays, and so on) for most of her adult life. Now in her fifties, Susanne shared that she had been drinking her two glasses of wine with dinner with her husband. After he went to bed, she would have another glass, sometimes two. Susanne would leave just enough in the bottle so that there wasn't an empty in the trash in the morning. She also rationalized the progression of her use by telling herself that she didn't finish the whole bottle. One night, after her fourth glass of wine, she fell and hit her head on the coffee table. While she was lucky and didn't need stitches, the fall sparked a conversation with her husband, and she tried to cut back. He shared that he had been worried about her consumption for a while and didn't know how to bring it up to her. He had mentioned how quickly they were going through wine, and whenever he brought it up, Susanne got angry and defensive. He chose to avoid the topic, hoping it would get better, and kept quiet. Susanne's husband was relieved that she wanted to cut down, not knowing that it isn't always possible to cut down on one's own use.

Things were better for a week, and when the drinking went back to four glasses a day, Susanne's husband became angry and frustrated. Their relationship was so fractured that Susanne felt that there was no reason to hide her drinking, and she started earlier and drank more every night. Then came the hangovers. In the mornings they were so debilitating that Susanne started missing work. Then she realized that the old pain pills made the hangovers go away more quickly. After her stash ran out, she searched the internet for a way to get pills without a prescription. At the thought of the danger and the legalities of her desperate measure, she became scared enough and had enough to lose (her husband and job) that she emailed a family member who had been to treatment in the past. Susanne's cousin passed along my contact details, and when we spoke, she said that that there had been enough changes in her drinking that the impact on her life was beginning to frighten her. It was important to Susanne that she get help before work got involved and she risked losing a job she loved. I recommended that she seek detox and ultimately residential treatment. She agreed, and we called the treatment center together to begin the process.

Asking for help doesn't have to be a grand, formal gesture. It can come in the form of what Susanne did—calling someone who has been there. Other ways to ask for help include the following:

- Mentioning to a family member that you are considering making a change.

  "Hey, Mom, I'm looking at cutting back on weed every day and thinking about getting back into yoga."
- Asking a friend or family member how your drinking and/or drug use has impacted them.

  "Hey Mom, I know that my being high has caused me to miss a lot of time with you. Is there anything else that has impacted you because of my being high?"
- Telling a friend or family member that you have tried to cut down and you can't.

  "Hey Mom, I've tried to cut back on my weed, and I just can't do it. I'm feeling scared."
- Acknowledging to a friend or family member that you aren't the only one who has needed help.

  "Hey Mom, remember when Dad went to the doctor and got some medication to help him with his drinking? I think I need something similar."
- Expressing curiosity about a sober lifestyle.

  "Hey, Mom, can we find out more about that sober dorm at my college or see what the Sober Young People group at church is about? I need new friends."

- Reading a book like *Quit Like a Woman* or picking up this book.

  "Hey, Mom, I heard about this really cool book. Do you want to read it together?"
- Expressing fears over our thoughts, actions, or a specific event.

  "Hey, Mom, I blacked out last night after the party, and I don't want to do that again."

Choosing Who You Ask for Help

Susanne's experience shows three different approaches to asking for help. Susanne started with her partner, then a family member who had been through treatment who suggested a behavioral health professional (me), who then suggested a treatment center. There are various inflection points or progressions (like the fall and trying to cut back on her own) and life circumstances that informed her decision on whom to ask.

For instance, early in her story, there was the feeling that she could handle it on her own (control as inflection point one). She admitted to the secret drinking that contributed to her fall and accepted her husband's encouragement to cut back (inflection point two). When Susanne realized that she was unable to control her drinking and she could lose her husband, who was frustrated and angry, she reached out to a family member in recovery (inflection point three). Suzanne's family member quickly involved a behavioral health professional. If you don't have a family member with lived experience, a trusted person in recovery, teachers, clergy, medical professionals, and recovery groups (they have been through it), are also options to provide support.

Asking for help is courageous not weak, and being honest about lying and hiding is important. So often we think our family members are too tired and angry to help and that isn't so. You may find that when you ask, as Dr. Zhao concluded, they will be relieved and ready to support. What if you find yourself in a situation where you feel that there is no one to turn to? You're in a new city, your family is out of the question, you don't trust therapists, and you don't have a doc you feel comfortable with. Please don't despair. There are online resources available in blogs, podcasts, and even virtual support group meetings. While it may sound overwhelming, going to a local 12-step meeting and saying that you are a newcomer looking for support will provide the instant community and connection you need.

Depending on who you decide to ask, there are different approaches to take. In Susanne's case, she reached out to her family member via email. Perhaps she wanted to take her time and read over her words, choosing them carefully and revising as she saw fit, until she felt comfortable committing to them. Other people might have more of a direct personality and choose to meet face-to-face so they could read physical cues and be more interactive. It is also a good idea to think of two or three different people that you can ask. We don't want to count on one person and then be disappointed if they aren't available or willing. Picking up the phone or meeting face-to-face is ideal, however, that isn't always practical due to schedules and distance. Some people don't even answer their phones anymore. Emails and letters are often effective and allow you to reach out to a few people with one approach. Regardless of who you choose to ask for help, it's important to craft your ask in a way that shows three important aspects:

Specificity

Be clear in the behaviors that you want to change so the recipients are clear. We don't want to make assumptions that they know what we want to change. Also, be clear in what type of help you are asking for.

Genuineness

Your reader may feel that they have heard it before and question your sincerity. Do your best to express sincere regret and desire for help.

Accountability

Own your past behaviors and regrets. Be clear about what you are willing to do differently, for example, going to treatment, getting drug testing, or ending relationships.

Here is a sample letter that hits all the marks.

> *Dear Cousin / Doc / Priest / Dentist / Supervisor,*
>
> *I know that you are busy right now, and I apologize in advance for dumping this on you.*
>
> *My drinking has increased to the point that I am really scared, and I have also been taking pain pills for hangovers* [specific]. *I can't stop on my own and I need help* [accountable]. *I want to*

> *put my life back together. I know that you have been through something similar, and I'm asking for your help* [genuine]. *Will you support me in finding a therapist who will work with me to help me figure out what I need? I am willing to do anything to get better. Please let me know if this is something that you can do.*

Always ask at the end of your request if they are willing to help. That is the goal. If they are not willing or you do not hear back from them, then move to the next person on your list. Someone's lack of agreement to help is often a reflection of their own substance use and has nothing to do with you. Move quickly and process later.

In the following circumstances, it is not effective to ask for help:

1. When under the influence (either you or your family member).
2. Over text (timing is everything and let's face it—texts can be intrusive).
3. During emotionally charged holiday celebrations. ("How can you let me get this bad? Help!") In fact, asking for help *before* the holidays is wise.
4. Making veiled threats. ("If you don't help me, I'm going to off myself.")
5. Asking for money. ("If you want me to do this, I'll need to borrow money from you to pay for treatment.")
6. Bringing up their use. ("Even though your drinking is worse than mine, I need help.")

7. Making secrecy a condition. ("I need to go to rehab. Don't tell Mom, or I won't go.")

Work It!

Make a list of potential people to ask for help. Use rigorous honesty! (Don't look for the easy way out, a.k.a. denial.)

Professionals—who are the doctors, therapists, nurses in my life?

Family members—who has energy to help me without making it about them?

Recovery community—do I know anyone in recovery? Or is it easier to ask a stranger?

For Fans and Family: What to Make of Interventions

Calling an intervention for a loved one is one of the most loving and supportive actions that you can take. We've spent some time discussing the denial that your loved one might be exercising, which often is what led your loved one to call for an intervention. If you have called an interventionist, it's because of the following:

- You have compassion for your loved one's situation.
- You have tried other interventions that have failed (clergy, family, and so on).

- You are frightened.
- You are ready to take the risk that your loved one will stop talking to you.
- You would rather attend your loved one's intervention than their funeral.
- You need more support and family coaching.

If you don't understand the process of intervention, professional interventionists are specially trained and able to immerse themselves into the family dynamics and provide 100 percent of their attention to that family with the shared goal of getting a loved one into treatment. This is much different than calling a therapist, who will likely not make house calls or be present to mediate between family members.

When a loved one is out of resources or ideas, and family or therapeutic interventions haven't worked, it is time to hire an intervention professional. Frustration, overwhelm, and fear are usually very high when this step is taken. Therapists will also call an interventionist for the same reason. I recently enlisted the services of an interventionist for a former client who was in denial about her relapse and the impact it was having on her physical health. This compassionate interventionist stepped in to create a "board of directors" of concerned individuals that would support the family. Through education, coaching, implementation of boundaries, and many other strategies, the client agreed to go to treatment. The intervention was a process—not an event—and it saved her life. In this context, however, an intervention is planned carefully by family, friends, and professionals.

It is always recommended to utilize a trained and certified intervention professional (ARISE and certified intervention professional, or CIP, are a few well regarded credentials). Interventionists are trained to help diffuse any anger and frustration that your loved one may project during the intervention and help keep the focus on the loved one's need to get help rather than any other dysfunction in the family system.

Through the process of intervention with education and support and regardless of if your loved one goes to treatment or not, the family system is forever changed. In that sense, every intervention is successful.

How Does a Typical Intervention Work?

An intervention is not necessarily a confrontation. If properly planned and executed, it becomes a "carefrontation," showing the compassion and support that that is available to the person struggling. A successful intervention will be planned carefully and tailored to the unique needs of the circumstances. As a loved one, you may read letters you wrote sharing how the person's addiction has impacted their life. You will express your desire that your person get help because they are loved and missed. You will also set a boundary explaining what will happen if your person doesn't get help. For example, "If you continue to use, then I will take care of myself and end the relationship." A highly individualized and well-run intervention empowers you to make changes before things get worse. It's also a chance for the person struggling to accept help.

As a key part of the intervention, it is imperative that you ask for a decision right away. Don't give your loved one time to think about whether to accept help, even if they want a few days to think it over. Delaying treatment allows time for dangerous behaviors to "wobble" (when self-doubt and inner critics set in) on the part of the family and be manipulated. It is nearly impossible to be reasonable with someone caught in the grips of substance use or psychiatric crisis.

Unfortunately, not all interventions end with the person going to treatment. In some cases, your loved one with an addiction may not accept the treatment plan. They may get very angry or say that help isn't needed. They also may be resentful and accuse you of betrayal or hypocrisy. "Not today" doesn't mean "never," and it's important to stay the course.

"'Not today' doesn't mean 'never,' and it's important to stay the course."

Emotionally prepare yourself for these situations, however, remain hopeful for positive change. Even if your loved one doesn't accept treatment at this time, be prepared to follow through with the changes you presented. Ask other people involved to join you in making the adjustments in their behavior that will support recovery.

Play 3. Overcome Your Emotions After an Intervention

This book opened with a discussion on where you might be when it comes to asking for help. This was not an attempt to coerce you into a decision you are not ready to make. It was included to raise your awareness of some of the mechanisms you might have put in place unknowingly that are keeping your bag of rocks heavy and burdensome. Just reading some of these pages may have already made you uncomfortable, stirring emotions that make you want to shove away or set this book on fire. Or perhaps, someone has intervened on your behalf or held up a mirror that you don't want to stare into. You may be angry, confused, frustrated, or ashamed. Or, you may be feeling alone and isolated after someone you trusted didn't answer your email asking for help. There are many variables to consider on this journey, which is why before we move on, the last play of this chapter is to validate these emotions so that you can manage them and not let them fuel your addiction or impulsively sway you away from getting the treatment you may need.

> *I'm angry and resentful!*
>
> You may be angry at God that you have to go through this and wonder if after everything, will there still be a positive outcome. These emotions are all completely expected when going through a trauma like an addiction.
>
> *Advice:* Whether you've been intervened or ignored, approaching your loved one's point of view with compassion and empathy can help you come to a place of acceptance. If you've been intervened, think about how your loved ones were coming from a place of love. This will be an important first step in mending relationships. If your request for help has been unanswered or turned down, ask yourself—what is it like to be them? Should you worry that they are suffering in their own life? Could it be possible they don't believe in themselves enough to help you? In any case, it's important not to view this as a judgment. Rather, view it as a reflection that they are not the right person to help you at this time.

I feel like a fool! I've been pretending that I'm okay, and after reading about denial, it is so obvious to everyone that I'm lost.

Advice: Your ego is not helping you right now. You cannot get into other people's heads and know that's what they think. In my experience, family and friends are relieved when everyone is on the same page. If you feel lost, your family now knows that you are looking for a map back to them and your life.

I am so sad and regretful. I blew up at the intervention, but I want my family back.

Advice: It's okay to express regret over your behavior and your desire to keep the relationship alive—even if you don't know exactly what that looks like in this moment. No relationship should be defined on its worst day. Think about your relationship before the disease of addiction and feel the love that was there. Be grounded in the trust of that relationship and let that guide you to speak with honesty and openness. A clean slate is possible after an intervention. If you need to take some time before you speak, that's okay too. Sometimes emotional distance or being cut off is the answer for now, and that's fine. Don't make any rash decisions.

I'm scared and want to stop this journey.

Advice: Remember that change doesn't just happen; it's a process. Understanding which stage of change you are in (there are many) will help you know yourself more deeply and gently guide you to the next stage until ultimately you will find that you are ready (or at least willing), without having to hit rock bottom first. We will discuss stages of change in the next chapter.

CHAPTER 2

EXAMINING YOUR MINDSET

The Plays for Understanding the Stages of Change

"There is no moment of delight in any pilgrimage like the beginning of it."

—CHARLES DUDLEY WARNER

You're probably wondering why the beginning plays in a rehab playbook concern things like the coping mechanisms we just discussed in the last chapter. In any challenge, the game is mostly a mental one, and these first two chapters guide you to consider the different aspects of how you can mentally prepare for the road ahead. What are the things that strengthen your mindset as you prepare for this journey, and what are the culprits that detract from making the change? Both questions are important to answer so you can take the next steps in deciding which treatment form(s) is/are appropriate, as well as work with others to support you in your recovery journey.

One of the most pervasive occurrences in the recovery world is also a well-known term in the current vernacular:

"rock bottom." According to The Substance Abuse and Mental Health Services Administration, rock bottom is what facilitates movement toward change.

The reason we begin with this concept is because rock bottom is both a driver and a detractor of adopting a recovery mindset. Rock bottom is typically a point in a person's life when their addiction has directly caused devastating circumstances that negatively impact their life and/or the life of someone else. Rock bottom can be a watershed moment when a person finally decides to get help. It is a point where a person with a substance use disorder admits that they have nothing left to lose and feels the worst that they have ever felt.

Getting to rock bottom can incite feelings of shame, hopelessness, loss, demotivation, isolation, worthlessness, and feeling stuck (to name only a few negative feelings), all of which sometimes makes it harder for a person to get help, keeping them in their addiction. They are too ashamed to ask for help or too "far gone" to think that they can make a change.

While rock bottom is a very real thing, the idea of "waiting for rock bottom" before one seeks help is a myth. The myth is supported by our defense mechanisms, like rationalization and minimalization, to think that it is *only* rock bottom that justifies our treatment. Waiting to hit rock bottom is a high-risk play as all defense mechanisms discussed in chapter 1 can be in full force while waiting to crash land. Denial, minimization, blaming—all of them. Often, treatment is postponed because a person thinks, "I can't be at my rock bottom because I can still work" or "I live in a million-dollar home; does this look like a rock bottom to you?" Family members who wait for their loved ones to hit rock bottom are also playing with fire.

In part, rehabilitation is about teaching people to change their behavior and seek help for their addictions. Early addiction research suggested that for this to happen, a person needed to experience consequences that were oftentimes terrible and beyond repair—a.k.a. rock bottom. But now, as there is more acceptance of substance use disorder as a disease, and less stigma and shame around it, rock bottom can be considered a turning point. When the thought of things staying as they are is more frightening than the fear of change.

> ***"Waiting to hit rock bottom is a high-risk play as all defense mechanisms discussed in chapter 1 can be in full force while waiting to crash land. Denial, minimization, blaming—all of them."***

We shift our perspective from one having to free fall and crash into a hard and dangerous surface to one of having an awareness of a moment that offers insight about the consequences of an addiction. These turning points are opportunities to pivot and enter a new stage of change. Learning to enter a mindset that can be more open to these turning point moments instead of waiting to crack our heads open on a hard surface is one of the goals of this chapter. Might you come to treatment earlier if you weren't waiting around for the worst thing that could happen?

Play 1. Look for Turning Points

Just like the concept of rock bottom, your turning point is just that—*yours*. It is subjective and differs from person to person.

Rock bottom for one person could be a fatal car accident while for another person it could be forgetting a parent-teacher conference. In any case, it is typically an eye-opening or startling event that motivates a person toward change and to seek treatment. As the saying goes, "The hardest thing that's ever happened to you is the hardest thing that's ever happened to you." So don't let the turning point moment fool you into thinking it's not *bad enough*.

Your turning point, just like rock bottom, is an event that motivates you to seek treatment. But it doesn't have to be a negative event, necessarily. Sometimes you might have a small win that boosts your confidence and keeps you motivated for the next win, like finding out you are going to be a parent or grandparent.

There are many significant moments or events that mark a shift or change that motivate you to take positive action. Identifying turning points in your life map to the stage of change you might be in is also important to understand as you consider rehabilitation. Sometimes turning points can be subtle or unexpected. John, who used painkillers for three years, had experienced work-related problems, impaired memory, and even stole money once from a close friend. But it wasn't until that friend said to him, "You love drugs more than you love your baby girl," that he had a deep moment of insight. That was his turning point, and he sought treatment. Twelve years later, he is still in recovery and has a special relationship with his now-teenage daughter.

According to many treatment programs and research, there are different ways turning points can manifest. Keep an eye out for these in your own experience:

A wake-up call: Sally woke up and saw her fender was dented. Did she hit something last night after the work happy hour? Is her blackout causing her to not remember something dire that happened as she drove home intoxicated? This event of a near-miss showed Sally that there was a potential major consequence to her addiction. The urgency of making a change became apparent.

A new insight: Like the example with John, a new insight could be a circumstance that causes someone to gain a new perspective or understanding about their substance use or its impact on their life or the life of others, causing a shift in their mindset or attitude.

A source of support: I've seen the power of when a person connects with a supportive community. Whether it be a recovery group or a private counselor, knowing you are not alone and also how many other people struggle with substance use disorder can provide encouragement to further seek guidance.

A small success: Before seeking treatment, Don, an insurance salesman with a fondness for vintage cars and Pabst Blue Ribbon, pledged he would only drink two beers at the Super Bowl party. Despite the temptation to join the gang when shots were poured, he kept his pledge. This was his moment when his small progress felt very significant. This punch in the arm showed him that he was capable of reaching a milestone, which gave him motivation to continue on the path to recovery.

Play 2. Admit You Hit Rock Bottom

Now that we have opened your mind to other ways that you can be inspired and motivated to seek treatment, we cannot overlook the reality of rock bottom.

When someone has a lot of resources, it will take longer to hit bottom. A former client of mine had relapsed on cocaine shortly after being discharged from treatment. He had access to endless dollars in the form of a trust fund, so his cocaine and escorts were delivered to his home. He was not open to returning to treatment and was skipping out on his drug tests mandated by the trust. While all of his bills were paid by the trust, his family ignored the signs and let the drug tests slide. He could have gone on for years until his rock bottom hit. Because I was authorized to

Circle of Support

As a brand-new therapist, fresh out of grad school in Phoenix, Arizona, there were a few options for jobs. We could work on the crisis unit in a psych hospital (which I had done in my internship), do evening groups for folks getting out of prison on drug charges, or do assessments at a methadone clinic. As I was drawn to addiction work, it was an easy choice to do the evening groups and assessments. On my first day, I was thrilled about finally calling myself a therapist *and* getting a paycheck. So I bounded into the waiting room of the methadone clinic. There was a man sitting in the chair near the door, eyes down, clutching a grocery bag. The bag, as I learned, contained all his earthly belongings. I put out my hand and said, "Hi, I'm Jaime." He gave me a perplexed look and lifted his shaking hand to mine. As I shook it and looked into his eyes, I could see the years of suffering and pain. He whispered that his name was Sam.

Later that day, Sam was in the group I was cofacilitating. He told me I was the first person in over a year to look him in the eyes and offer to touch him, other than in anger or to steal something. Sam enrolled in the methadone program, got some clean time in, and I learned about the power of simple things in restoring someone's dignity. Everything matters.

have regular calls with the trust, we had a family meeting and decided to bring his rock bottom to him. What that means is that the trustee told him that if he would not go to treatment, they would pull his monthly allotment, take his vehicle, and evict him from his apartment. Being used to his comforts, he agreed to treatment. This all took several weeks, and while we were working through the process of setting boundaries, he was able to access plenty of cash to fund his lifestyle and there was no rock bottom.

Waiting for rock bottom is dangerous which is why it's important to look for your turning points. Although rock bottom is different for everyone, certain situations may become watershed moments when you realize that you need to make a change:

- When you got busted for being high at work and were at risk of losing your license.
- The first time that you woke up naked, blacked out, and didn't know where you were or how you got there.
- When you stole medications from your dying parents (this is a very common occurrence).
- Serving prison time after three DUIs—because the first two DUIs were not enough.
- When you lived on the streets and traded sex for drugs.

Work It!

What is your rock bottom? Ask yourself, "What am I willing to lose?" There is a group exercise done in treatment where the clients write down the three things that are most important to them. Most often it's a combination of their partner, children, career, and pets. The facilitator goes around the circle and, one by one, each person must give up one of the three things, until finally they are left with nothing. As a metaphor for addiction taking everything from us, this exercise creates a great deal of stress and anger, with clients clinging to their last treasured card.

List here the three things in your life that are most important to you in order of importance. Don't forget to include yourself.

1. ______________________________
2. ______________________________
3. ______________________________

Imagine each of these being taken from you one by one. How does this make you feel? What is your heart doing? Are your palms sweaty? Do you feel angry, or do you not want to go further with the exercise? These are all important emotions to feel to determine that this loss is not something you want to or even could endure.

Play 3. See Yourself in the Stages of Change

Even with turning points and rock bottoms, sometimes a person doesn't make the choice to seek treatment. As humans, we all have habits and behaviors that we would like to change, but change is difficult, whether quitting smoking, exercising more, or reducing stress.

Why is change so difficult? Well, for starters, change isn't a one-time event. It's a process. In 1992, the transtheoretical model of change (a.k.a. "stages of change") was developed out of research done by James Prochaska and Carlo DiClemente. It is called "transtheoretical" because the model is derived from several different theories and concepts from psychology. This model is frequently applied to addiction. Understanding the stages of change can be helpful for individuals who want to understand their overwhelming feelings about changing their behaviors and for health professionals who work with clients or patients. By identifying which stage of change a person is in, interventions can be tailored to meet their specific needs and increase the likelihood of success.

"By identifying which stage of change a person is in, interventions can be tailored to meet their specific needs and increase the likelihood of success."

How many times has a loved one asked you to stop? Why don't you? Nobody likes to be told what to do and to be treated as if they have no choices. Whether it's a change like deciding to go to treatment or simply eating more healthfully, hearing "just do it or else" will not motivate us to make the change. In many cases, it can backfire and cause the opposite result. The saying "the student must be ready" is relevant when we think about where we are when it comes to even making the first step toward making a change. This typically is what frustrates family members, especially when an intervention isn't effective. They want to know why their loved one won't do what they say or ask of them or at the very least admit to their behavior. When we approach another's need to change with expectations or demands, when it should be instead approached with empathy, it just doesn't work.

Identifying or being aware of the several different stages of change is insightful as you learn more about your motivations, readiness, and level of commitment you want to take. It will also enlighten you as to how you move in and out of stages and what self-talk, triggers, or mindsets might be contributing to them. You will see how the defense mechanisms from the last chapter, as well as turning points, are exhibited in some of these stages as well. Not everyone will progress linearly through each stage. We may move back and forth between stages or even skip stages altogether. This is normal and expected.

Precontemplation

In a talk I gave to union employees, I shared the definition of binge drinking, which is, according to the National Institute on Alcohol Abuse and Alcoholism, five or more drinks in two hours for men and four or more drinks in two hours for women. This seemed to disturb one of the men in the crowd, "John," who raised his hand and aggressively challenged me, saying, "I drink that much each week, and my relationships are fine, and I'm healthy."

Others in the audience shared their experience with the alcohol overdose of some of their colleagues, one of which was intimated was John. Until this point, John may have lacked knowledge and education about the negative health consequences and risk potential of binge drinking. This also may have brought up feelings of hopelessness about quitting, believing that he will never be able to have fun without drinking. He didn't take all of this lightly, and while we don't know if this education was beneficial to him or not, I like to think that we planted a seed and at least an openness to listen. In the precontemplation stage, we

- might not see our behaviors as problems,
- might lack the understanding of the consequences of our actions; and
- might need education and resources to enlighten us more about the effects of our behaviors and to know change is possible.

Emotion(s): Denial is used as a defense mechanism avoid negative feelings.

Self-talk: "No one understands me, and everyone is blowing things out of proportion."

Remember: Someone in the precontemplation stage may need more time to be ready and willing to listen about the benefits of change. Fear of rock bottom alone doesn't do it since in the precontemplation stage the addictive voice says that a bad situation will never happen to them. It is often necessary to wait until a person is ready to move to the next stage before attempting to persuade them to change their behavior.

Contemplation

The giveaway that John was still in the precontemplation stage was that he argued with me. If he were in the contemplation stage, he would've remained quiet, listening to what we all had to say and absorbing it and really thinking about it. John's self-reflection would have included times that his drinking had caused issues, and perhaps he would be thinking about what a sporting event could look like sober. He might wonder if he would still enjoy his golf weekends with his friends. He would potentially make a note to check out what hours the employee assistance program counselor had in the office; however, he would continue with his usual plans for the coming weekend.

When we reach the contemplation stage, we

- consider changing our behavior and
- may weigh the pros and cons of changing and consider the advantages and disadvantages of our current behavior.

Emotion(s): Conflicted: This stage can be challenging to navigate, as we may feel conflicted about whether we want to make a change.

Self-talk: "Maybe I did cause an issue last weekend with my drinking. It's scary with all of the fentanyl on the streets."

Remember: The contemplation stage can be challenging but necessary in making a change. By acknowledging our conflicted emotions and identifying potential barriers to change, we can take the necessary steps to move forward and progress toward our goals.

Preparation

John had a turning point moment and realized he had to make changes in his drinking. In the preparation stage, he made the promise to himself that this weekend he would stop at two drinks, gathering information about the health benefits of cutting down. He created a plan for when his buddies encouraged him to have a third, fourth, or fifth drink. He may also ask himself what was triggering the need to get loaded every weekend (usually his boss or feelings for his old girlfriend) and think about ways to avoid or manage them. Finally, he considered talking to someone in his employee assistance program for suggestions of support group resources to help him stay on track.

During the preparation stage we

- begin to look at what it would take to make these changes (I need to be aware of whether I am becoming impaired);
- gather information (learn how is alcohol metabolized), set goals (I will leave the bar before 10 p.m.), and create a plan of action (I will drink water in between drinks); and
- identify our readiness and ability to change and begin to identify any barriers that may prevent us from

achieving our goals (Am I able to cut down on my own without medical intervention?).

Emotion(s): Guilt: As we own the need to make a change, the ramifications of past behaviors will inevitably creep up.

Self-talk: "I can do this. I will feel better the next day if I stop at two drinks. It will be great not to spend the next day on the couch after a night out."

Remember: The preparation stage is essential to the behavior change process. We can increase our chances of success by setting goals, gathering information, creating a plan, identifying barriers, and building support.

Action

In the contemplation stage, John made the decision to cut down and gave it a sincere try. While he controlled his drinking one night, it was obvious to him that he was obsessing, irritable, and stressed the whole time. Moving into the action stage, he told his loved ones that he was getting help with stopping and that he had enrolled in a nighttime intensive outpatient program. He saw the negative impact that drinking had had on his life, especially when he would drink to avoid the feelings of sadness and loneliness from a recent breakup or running into his old girlfriend. He also planned to avoid people and places associated with drinking, and he tried and liked a 12-step meeting.

In the contemplation stage we

- commit to changing our behavior;

- actively take steps toward our goal (find an activity that isn't centered around alcohol, like sober softball or call our cousin in recovery, rather than calling a drinking buddy);
- acknowledge that our behavior is problematic, so we make specific plans for change and plans to deal with triggers (avoid places where alcohol is served and practice breathing and meditation when stressed or lonely); and
- seek support from friends and relatives.

Emotion(s): Relief: Often there are lies and risky behaviors associated with use that are exhausting. Knowing that there is hope can be a load off.

Self-talk: "I can have fun sober." "I don't have to be numb to deal with my stress."

Remember: During the action stage, we are actively participating in our recovery. This stage can be challenging, but it is also where we can see the most progress. It is important to remember that change is a process, and setbacks can happen. Staying motivated and focused on our goal is essential, even if we experience setbacks. We can use our support system to help us stay on track and keep us accountable.

Maintenance Stage

After about two months of cutting alcohol out of his life entirely, John considered attending a sporting event with his old friends, where he would more than likely run into his ex-girlfriend. He was also thinking about cutting back to one 12-step meeting a week and started to smoke a little weed. When he ran all of these ideas past his sponsor, he was encouraged to stay the current course, keep working the plan that he had in place, and not take his eyes off the prize of sobriety.

In the maintenance stage, we

- have successfully changed our behavior and are now focusing on maintaining it;
- maintain the changes by consistently adhering to a routine and engaging with our support system; and
- implement strategies to avoid triggers.

Emotion(s): Gratitude and confidence: In early recovery, we may find ourselves so happy about our new life that we become complacent in doing the things that we know are helpful.

For Fans and Family

Research suggests that up to 90 percent of interventions succeed at getting the person into treatment. That's encouraging. Treatment, however, is the ticket to the movie, not the movie. The question of whether your loved one will find and maintain a lifestyle of sustained recovery is dependent on a variety of factors, including the amount of effort that is put forth in relapse prevention for your loved one and family. If we think of interventions with the stages of change model in mind, we find that we are often taking someone from the precontemplative stage and fast forwarding them into the action phase—or else.

Most times, this large of a leap can be facilitated by skillful treatment center staff who basically do a crash course in contemplation and preparation with the patient until they catch up in their stage. Other times, it is a bridge too far, and although a person accepted the offer of treatment, they leave treatment against medical advice. This once again reinforces the importance of finding a treatment center that is experienced in working with interventionists and learning their treatment completion rates with patients who are admitted after an intervention.

Stages of Change of Friends and Family

Fans and family members also go through their own stages of change process, and that's ok. Keep in mind that your rock bottom may look very different than your loved ones. In a perfect world, the stages of changes would be a parallel process, and we would all joyfully skip through them hand in hand at the same time. Not in my experience. Effective family therapy intervention will be geared toward the family's stage of recovery, and this stage may or may not parallel their loved one's motivation for change or actual changed behavior. If you are a fan or family member, see if any of the information below resonates.

Stage	Family Member Voice
Precontemplative	This isn't our problem. We have had enough blame by "experts."
Contemplative	Assessment was "BS." Some of it did ring true. Still mad at "experts."
Preparation	I can't take it anymore. My life is in shambles—what can I do?
Action	His being sober is a big change for our family. Do we have to quit drinking?
Maintenance	I'm going to get healthy too. I would love having my own therapist.

Self-talk: "I got this. I don't need to really do ninety meetings in ninety days." "My family is so thrilled with me; they won't care if I skip a meeting."

Remember: The maintenance stage is about staying focused and committed to our new behavior. This means continuing to work your plan and avoiding the people, places, and things that are triggering. The main detractors from focus are complacence, in other words not doing what you know works and a sense of being bullet proof. This stage is crucial because it helps us to prevent relapse and solidify our new habits. It is all too common for a false sense of confidence to creep in, and we put ourselves in high-risk situations without a plan.

Relapse Stage

John had six months of sobriety. With the help of his sponsor, he was working his program, had new friends, and played on a sober softball team. He had also stopped convincing himself that smoking a little weed here and there wasn't so bad. Then he got the news. His former girlfriend was engaged. He immediately went to a bar and proceeded to drink shots of whiskey. Realizing that he had made a mistake, he called his sponsor and went to a meeting the next day. He also agreed to re-enroll in his nighttime intensive outpatient program. He was grateful that his relapse was a slip and didn't lead him back to his old behavior. What he realized was that he had a lot more work to do to process the toll that the end of his relationship with his old girlfriend had on him. He also needed to plan support for the weekend of her wedding.

Relapse is a normal part of any change process or chronic disease. This is especially important in substance use recovery because relapse can be life threatening. Relapse can be a frustrating and discouraging experience, but it is essential to remember that it is not a failure. It means that we have more work to do on our plan of care. A relapse can be a slip where we don't go back to regular use. We learn, recover, and get back on the proverbial horse even stronger than before.

Some things that happen in relapse are

- loss of motivation;
- return to old patterns of behavior; and
- not recognizing the early warning signs that you are triggered.

Emotion(s): Shame, fear, and hopelessness arise when facing perceived failure of relapse.

Self-talk: "I don't know who I thought I was fooling." "I might as well keep drinking."

Remember: Relapse can begin long before you pick up a drink or drug. It begins when you stop working your plan and go back to old behaviors. Knowing your relapse behaviors (what you look and feel like when you are in trouble) and empowering a few supportive loved ones to hold up a mirror can prevent relapse or get you back on track immediately.

Work It!

Understanding triggers and recognizing your own is essential. Triggers are emotional, environmental, or social situations (people, places, and things) that stir up emotions that can create an impulse to use a substance or other unhealthy coping mechanism. Triggers do not necessarily lead to relapse; however, they may make it more difficult to resist the impulses that they produce. More positively, triggers create early warning signs that signal what you look and feel like when things aren't going well. This awareness is an important part of relapse prevention planning.

The following are some common substance use relapse triggers. Think about how these apply to you and rate them 1-5, with 5 being the truest.

Do I feel triggered when I am:

Hungry, angry, lonely, or tired?

___

Feeling guilt or sadness?

___

Idealizing or embellishing the positives of the past (alcohol, drugs, or relationship)?

___

Feeling overconfident in my recovery?

___

On social media?

___

Thinking about my job or profession?

___

Seeking and Accepting Help

Help comes in different forms at different times in our lives. It can be a well-intentioned family member, a coworker, clergy, or our medical professional. In an ideal world, we have gone through our stages of change and are in the action stage, and our loved one responds exactly as we have hoped. When a family member tries too soon or waits too long due to their estrangement or their own use, it can have a negative outcome.

For loved ones and friends, watching someone hit rock bottom or careen toward it is a traumatic and terrifying life event. When they are out of ideas and resources, there are intervention professionals that can step in to help. The next chapter outlines the various treatment forms and options while we consider how our personal needs and levels of substance use disorder dictate the plan we choose (or chooses us).

CHAPTER 3

DECIDING YOUR PLAYING FIELD

The Plays for Choosing Appropriate and Effective Care

"One of the hardest things was learning that I was worth recovery."

—DEMI LOVATO

Often unintentionally, many people still talk about addiction in ways that are stigmatizing—meaning that they use words that can portray someone with substance use disorder (SUD) in a shameful or negative way. Using the terms "drug addicts," "junkie," "drunk," "dirty," or "clean" rather than "SUD" or "person suffering from SUD" can increase shame and reluctance to ask for help as they feel that they are not worthy. With simple changes in language, harmful stigma and negativity around SUD can begin to fade away, making it a more comfortable conversation. If you are wondering if you are an alcoholic or drug addict, I encourage you to reframe such labels because SUD is a chronic and treatable disorder.

The substantial shift in understanding the nature of addiction as a chronic rather than an acute (short duration) illness or a moral failure has changed social perceptions, substance use prevention, treatment, and outcome expectations. SUD is no longer thought of (by most) as a moral failing, character flaw, or something that someone has to just "say no" to. Through the hard work of the medical community and industry advocacy, we now know that chronic, relapsing disorders of SUD are diseases from which people can recover and lead productive lives through long-term treatment, continuing care, and recovery support.

Identifying your SUD means that you are activating the stages of change discussed in chapter 2 and engaging in the beginnings of an important conversation: What kind of treatment do I need? Which will be the most effective and appropriate? And what are my goals for treatment?

There is no one-size-fits-all method when it comes to our health. Chronic disease management requires action in all life domains. Integrating treatments that treat issues of the whole person—mind, body, and spirit—is widely accepted and encouraged in today's treatment climate. If a SUD is like a chronic health disorder such as heart disease, consider that getting back on your feet after a heart attack requires a healthy diet, exercise plan, reduction in stress, and so on. Depending on the severity of the heart damage and what skills you need to build, recovery can consist of minor changes or be as invasive and drastic as getting a pacemaker or having open heart surgery. Some patients may go to cardiac rehab, while some go back to their workout at the gym.

Treatment and recovery from SUD is no different. It is common, even typical, for people to utilize different methods of treatment over different periods of their life, depending on other life factors such as level of commitment, stage of change, family and financial support, consequences of use, and co-occurring disorders. Sometimes people's life circumstances cause them to take a different treatment path than professionally recommended; however, the lack of ability to follow a clinical recommendation does not always indicate that the patient is treatment resistant. There's a host of reasons and concerns even the most eager person has, ranging from childcare to work duties to finances—all legitimate concerns. However, these concerns arise because we tend to have one idea—the most drastic idea—of rehabilitation: residential care.

When people think of an addiction treatment facility, commonly known as "rehab," they likely envision an environment where patients sleep at the center and participate in group therapy led by kindly, wise therapists who also live on the premises. Hollywood has produced several movies addressing addiction, recovery, and life in and after rehab. Although not always accurate, these films provide drama, entertainment, and valuable insights. The movie *28 Days*, starring Sandra Bullock, depicts the "typical" rehab experience. It is even used as "movie therapy" in some treatment centers as part of the program.

This chapter is all about exploring the options available to you while considering the level of care you need—and a residential treatment is one of several options. Recovery care consists on a continuum and the term "continuum of care" refers to all levels of substance use treatment, from the most to the least intensive and restrictive. Simply put, from detox to hospitalization to outpatient services, the degree of care, delivery of care, and cost of care exist on a continuum. It is not only the goal of treatment providers to make sure that the care you receive keeps you safe and addresses all risks but also that the care is as "least intensive" as possible, which helps you avoid unnecessary or wasteful treatment.

It sounds like a simple concept, but I cannot tell you how often people overlook the options available to them, seeing only residential care. Or how many well-intentioned care providers see someone's unwillingness to go to residential treatment as a sign that they are not ready or even that they still need to hit their "rock bottom." It doesn't have to be all or nothing. This is important because starting at the nonresidential outpatient level of care allows you to address a concern before a crisis. For instance, if someone thinks that the only way that they can get sober is by going to rehab for thirty days, but they can't miss work or find childcare, they may keep using. Any treatment intervention is better than none.

"It doesn't have to be all or nothing."

To carry the metaphor of the playbook to the concept of knowing your options, just like a player's division, league, or position on the field is adjusted based on their level of play, people with SUD can, with the help of a support system, determine which playing field on the care continuum is possible or appropriate for them. When clinically appropriate, there are several options that are available—detox, residential treatment, partial hospitalization program, intensive outpatient programs, standard outpatient therapy, group therapy, and individual therapy.

Play 1. Know the Options

Many programs will help you to customize a plan that supports you holistically—mind, body spirit. We are physical, emotional, and spiritual beings. Our physical symptoms influence our emotions. Our emotions bring on physical symptoms. It is impossible to separate these coexisting conditions as they influence each other. I'm not suggesting that any one treatment center has the capability to "fix" your mind, body, and spirit, but a good program will begin the process of understanding where the emotional and physical pain points exist and work with you to create a comprehensive roadmap to address them throughout the continuum of care.

A good care plan also includes your job and your family relationships. For example, someone who is running a company or practicing medicine has different time constraints than someone who is retired. A single parent with school-age children has different availability than a stay-at-home parent whose partner is working full time. Finding the right fit for your care—whether a residential or outpatient program—also depends on the severity of your substance abuse challenges and whether you're also experiencing related medical or mental health complications. We will discuss your role, as well as your physician's role, in determining your risk level in Chapter Three: Deciding Your Playing Field: The Plays for choosing Appropriate and Effective Care.

The existence of co-occurring disorders is also crucial to examine and consider when weighing your rehabilitation options. According to the Substance Abuse and Mental Health Services Administration, "the co-existence of both a mental illness and SUD is known as a co-occurring disorder and is common occurrence among people in addiction treatment."

The Substance Abuse and Mental Health Services Administration's *2022 National Survey on Drug Use and Health* revealed that approximately 21.5 million adults in the United States have a co-occurring disorder. Over the past several years, it has been my experience that there has been an increase in the number of patients that present with one or more mental health disorders, while being addicted to one or more substances. A patient might be addicted to alcohol while suffering from depression, resulting in a suicide attempt. Another may be abusing prescription drugs to mask the emotional symptoms related to trauma. So, which comes first: the addiction or mental illness? Determining this and other factors associated with co-occurring disorders is explored at length in the next chapter.

For now, we should understand that the two main groups of treatment are residential and outpatient.

Residential

Residential treatment care (RTC) requires people to be in a twenty-four-hour sleepaway facility for a minimum of thirty days to a maximum of ninety. RTC is often referred to as a bubble because you are at the treatment center and supervised twenty-four hours a day, seven days a week. All your basic needs are met, and the world is kept at bay. This allows the therapeutic process to begin (six hours or more per day of programming) and healing to ensue without the constant barrage of social media, texts, voicemail, and relationship issues. A RTC program is a better fit if your SUD symptoms are severe or if you're struggling with co-occurring disorders such as depression, anxiety, or trauma.

Research shows that chances for success are best for those who remain in treatment for at least ninety days, but these days don't necessarily all need to be spent at the residential level. With that said, research shows good outcomes are contingent on adequate treatment length.

While there are common milestones in healing from addiction, your treatment and recovery path are your own—based on your specific situation, challenges, and needs. Like diabetes or hypertension, addiction is a chronic disease. Regaining and maintaining your health means learning to manage your symptoms, first within the structure and support of a treatment setting and eventually in your home environment where you're in charge of your sobriety.

When you successfully complete residential treatment, you will have a graduation ceremony and "coin out." This means that you receive a coin, chip, key chain, or some other memento to serve as positive reinforcement and a daily reminder to stay the course of sobriety. Your treatment team will have provided a recommendation for your continued care or step-down plan.

But First, Detox

Depending on the severity of SUD and substances involved, treatment often begins with a medically supervised detox, lasting anywhere from three to seven days. During detox, patients safely withdraw from their drug or drugs of choice. Since detox can be an unpleasant and dangerous process, it is always handled by qualified medical professionals.

Detox is for anyone who may be using drugs and/or alcohol on a prolonged basis. Detoxing on your own is high risk, so it's important that you get help from a medical professional.

There are stand-alone detox centers, detoxes within hospitals, and detoxes embedded in treatment centers. Often when detox is complete, a patient will say, "I'm good" and decide they don't need additional treatment. The relapse rate for the "detox only" option is much higher than for those who continue treatment. That said, if short-term management of alcohol or drugs is the only goal, a detox center can provide that. (Detox alone is not treatment.)

Regardless of your choice about where to detox, a plan for continued care and support will be vital to success if your goal is abstinence from drugs or alcohol. Detoxes employ knowledgeable clinicians who work with you to create the care plan that best meets your needs. Although many people experience mild withdrawal symptoms and may confuse withdrawal with something harmless, the outcome of withdrawal is unpredictable and potentially life threatening, which is why a medically supervised detox to manage withdrawal is essential.

Work It!

Determining your level of care relies on your personal goals for treatment. The prompts below are helpful as a personal reminder tool to write out your goals, prioritize them, and make a plan to see them through, whether they are to detoxify your body from the substances, seek an integrated treatment for coexisting emotional, spiritual, and physical issues, or connect with others in a community of people with similar goals.

Goal for Treatment:
Priority: (Low, Medium, High)
Plan to Get There: (Short term, long term)
Support Team:
Success looks like:

Outpatient and Step-Down Treatment Options

Most often, after completing residential treatment, the clinical recommendation is to "step down" to the lower level of care called a partial hospitalization program. However, the following outpatient treatment options are available regardless of seeking or receiving residential treatment.

Outpatient treatment is a type of behavioral health service designed to address physical, mental and emotional needs without overnight hospitalization. Outpatient treatment for substance abuse can be an ideal option if you have the motivation to get sober but can't take leave from work, disrupt school attendance, or step away from other responsibilities that would otherwise allow you to stay at a RTC. Please keep in mind that outpatient programs are designed to serve people with mild or moderate SUD symptoms.

If you are being referred by a medical professional, be in sync on this decision to ensure that your symptoms are a fit for outpatient treatment. (For example, if your primary care doctor says you need detox, it's not a good idea for you to insist on a virtual intensive outpatient program.) Your behavioral health professional will follow professional assessment criteria when determining your level of care, while your considerations might be more personal and less medically driven. The following are the outpatient options for levels of care from most intense to least.

- **Partial hospitalization programs:** This option requires therapy or counseling sessions four or five days per week, for six to eight hours per day, and are often offered with or without housing. Housing options consist of transitional or sober-living homes (more details in Chapter 12), which provide a semi-controlled environment where someone in recovery can dip their toe into reality. Ideally, a patient will stay in these programs for two to four weeks before stepping down to the less restrictive option of intensive outpatient.
- **Intensive outpatient programs:** This option requires attendance at therapy or counseling sessions several times a week, approximately three to four hours per day.
- **Standard outpatient programs:** This option requires attendance at therapy or counseling sessions one to two times per week, typically for one to two hours per session.
- **Group therapy:** This option requires attendance at sessions with other people in recovery.
- **Individual therapy:** This option requires one-on-one therapy or counseling with a trained professional.

Note: According to the Substance Abuse and Mental Health Services Administration's (Treatment Episode Data Set), the median length of rehab for drug addiction is as follows:

- Detox: 4 days
- Residential treatment (short-term): 27 days
- Intensive outpatient program: 88 days
- Outpatient treatment: 130 days
- Outpatient medication-assisted treatment for opioid therapy: 207 days

Play 2. Find Where You "Sit" on the SUD Continuum

According to the National Institute of Mental Health, "SUD is a treatable mental disorder that affects a person's brain and behavior, leading to their inability to control their use of substances like legal or illegal drugs, alcohol, or medications. Symptoms can be mild, moderate, or severe, with addiction being the most severe form of SUD." When seeking treatment, where one "fits" on the SUD continuum determines the care pathway. Let's explore how that works.

Behavioral health professionals work with a professionally designed diagnostic tool called *The Diagnostic and Statistical Manual of Mental Disorders*, 5th edition, or *DSM-5*, that provides diagnostic criteria for identifying SUDs. Specifically, knowing what the substance of use (often called drug of choice) is and how severe a SUD is (how much and how often for how long) will help physicians and SUD specialists determine the best course of treatment.

The *DSM-5* recognizes substance-related disorders related to the ten following drugs:

- Alcohol
- Caffeine
- Cannabis
- Hallucinogens
- Inhalants
- Opioids
- Sedatives
- Hypnotics
- Stimulants
- Tobacco

"According to the National Institute of Mental Health, 'SUD is a treatable mental disorder that affects a person's brain and behavior, leading to their inability to control their use of substances like legal or illegal drugs, alcohol, or medications.'"

It is not uncommon for substance use or misuse to exist in combinations of two or more drugs (for instance, alcohol and stimulants), which is called poly-substance use or misuse.

Behavioral health professionals rely on two significant tools in their work. First, as we just mentioned, is the *DSM-5*, which defines and classifies mental disorders and is used by clinicians to both diagnose and develop treatment recommendations for adolescents and adults. The other tool, the American Society of Addiction Medicine, provides a comprehensive set of guidelines for placement, continued stay, and transfer/discharge of patients with SUDs. Understanding both tools is an important step for these professionals in creating your playbook.

Work It!

Once the drug of choice is determined, your behavioral health professional will look at how and when the drug is used, despite negative effects. The *DSM-5* points out eleven criteria that can occur from substance use and misuse, falling into the categories of impaired control, physical dependence, social problems, and risky use. Take a look at the list and check off one or more symptoms that are true to your experience:

1. Using more of a substance than intended or using it for longer than you're meant to.
2. Trying to cut down or stop using the substance but being unable to.
3. Experiencing intense cravings or urges to use the substance.
4. Needing more of the substance to get the desired effect—also called tolerance.
5. Developing withdrawal symptoms when not using the substance.
6. Spending more time getting and using drugs and recovering from substance use.
7. Neglecting responsibilities at home, work, or school because of substance use.
8. Continuing to use even when it causes relationship problems.
9. Giving up important or desirable social and recreational activities due to substance use.

10. Using substances in risky settings that put you in danger.
11. Continuing to use despite the substance causing problems to your physical and mental health.

Like other illnesses, substance misuse worsens over time. The SUD criteria explained By utilizing the *DSM-5*, behavioral health professionals are able to discern the severity of an individual's SUD by determining the number of symptoms present. Some examples include the following:

- An *at risk* SUD individual may present with one symptom and would indicate that they be educated and made aware aware of their patterns of use.
- A *mild* SUD individual may present with two or three symptoms, which is a slight problem. While treatment may not be immediately necessary, symptoms worsen over time, so it is a good time to get support.
- A *moderate* SUD individual may present with Four or five symptoms and indicate that some treatment is recommended.
- A *severe* SUD individual may present with six or more symptoms, which signals an addiction to that substance and immediate need for treatment.
- Eight or nine symptoms mean that treatment is absolutely necessary, and you may have alcohol-related health issues as well.

When we understand where our use/misuse fits, then it is possible to explore our options with levels of care. We will now learn more about how the symptom criteria at the professional level reveal which level of care is most appropriate.

Play 3. Understand the Professional Assessment

A successful care plan will be created in collaboration between practitioner and patient. While it is the goal of treatment providers to make sure that the care you receive keeps you safe and addresses all risks, they will also recommend that the care is as "least intensive" as possible, which helps you avoid unnecessary or wasteful treatment. It is also important that you have your own goals for treatment in mind when you start the process.

You have learned how to review your own SUD levels and the options for treatment available, but it is quite helpful to understand how the professionals assess your level of care by considering the professional criteria they refer to in order to help them make the best recommendations for your risk level.

The assessment process is a critical component of determining the level of care. When seeking treatment, you should ensure that the program utilizes *The ASAM Criteria* in their assessment and looks at you holistically: mind, body, and spirit.

The ASAM Criteria was developed by the American Society of Addiction Medicine (ASAM) and presented in a book written by a group of renowned doctors and professionals. *ASAM*

For Fans and Family

As you and your loved ones weight the options available, the room is probably spinning and a million questions—and emotions—arise. If you decide on residential treatment, the following are important things to know about having a loved one in care:

Will I get to see my loved one?

Most treatment programs allow family members and friends to visit on a weekly basis. It is important that these visits are closely monitored and visitors are approved by the treatment team. Some centers will search the belongings of visitors, and while this may seem intrusive, it is done to ensure a safe environment.

Do I get to speak my mind?

Family involvement in the treatment process is another important factor to consider in weighing treatment options; however, it is important to note that collaboration on decision-making is critical. SUD impacts the entire family, and programs that offer comprehensive family therapy, education, support, and other resources are important. Through the family program, you will have the opportunity for all

Criteria is a set of detailed and objective guidelines that is used by Behavioral Health Professionals in treatment settings as a roadmap for treatment planning and determination of appropriate level of care. ASAM Criteria is also used by insurance companies to determine the number of days authorized at each level of care.

While recommending a level of care, a professional will ask themselves the following question: *How do I accurately document this to ensure maximum treatment coverage and to keep our patient safe?* While we will explore insurance coverage and the process in depth in the Chapter Four (Financial Facts and Impacts: The Play for Paying for Treatment), understanding the basics of *The ASAM Criteria* is an essential play.

The ASAM Criteria views patients as a whole person,

rather than a diagnosis. This means that, when recommending a level of care, *The ASAM Criteria* includes all of a person's life areas, as well as all risks, needs, strengths, and goals.

The "assessment" phase of treatment represents the early information-gathering phase, in which patient and physician work together to determine what signs and symptoms are present and what else might be going on in the patient's life. *The ASAM Criteria* begins this phase by asking, "What does the patient want?" and "Why now?" If there isn't an alignment between provider and patient and understanding on these early questions, it can significantly impact the later stages of treatment.

members of your family to work through feelings of regret, resentment, and appreciation, as well as set healthy boundaries to rebuild relationships.

Are they fixed?

The important point to remember when it comes to residential care, or "rehab," is that it's the ticket to the movie and not the movie itself. Many families believe that if their loved one puts in the time and money and goes to rehab, there will be a silver bullet cure and, voilà, they will get their loved one back. Nothing is further from the truth.

Recovery is a hard-fought battle requiring commitment from loved ones throughout treatment at all levels of care. It takes some people several treatment episodes, each experience building upon the other, before the pieces finally come together. The important thing is that the pieces can and do come together. Family healing happens every day.

There are six major life areas (or "dimensions") detailed in *The ASAM Criteria*, and each one impacts the others. Your treatment providers look at these dimensions from every angle, considering them separately and together, and exploring both risks and strengths in each.

Circle of Support

As a more experienced therapist in a "luxury" program, I was assigned to an angry, older man. Two therapists, a man and a woman, had refused to work with him because of his rage issues and foul language. I looked into his eyes, put out my hand, and introduced myself. He didn't say a word. I inquired, "What brings you into treatment?"

His reply, "My wife is a C#&%."

"We better get to work," I replied. Beneath the booze, anger, and frustration was one of the most insightful, talented, and wise humans I've ever met. This man was a famous singer/songwriter who was in immense emotional pain from becoming invisible to his young, successful wife and aging out of his profession. We worked with the man and his wife to put the pieces of their marriage back together. He realized she loved him but hated the disease of addiction.

Through a detailed explanation he shared, I learned that there are two types of folks: those who are the *singers* and those who are the *songs*. Singers are meant to perform in front of a crowd, carry the tune, and bring the music and lyrics to life to tell a story. Songs, on the other hand, love to hear others give voice to their creations. They provide the musical notes, the syncopation, and the poetry that becomes the lyrics.

Voilà! Things finally made sense to me, and for years, I have neatly organized my world into singers and songs. I have carefully included a balance of singers and songs when forming teams, hosting parties, and even within my own family. The man told me I was clearly operating as the song and should work on being more of a singer. His insight continues to shape my world view.

At his graduation from treatment, we shared how much meaning we had brought to each other's lives. He continued to bring meaning to my life by calling me on his sobriety date every year for ten years. He passed away at the age of eighty-four, sober and in a loving relationship with his wife. Everything matters.

TEAM MEETING

Interview with Bob Ferguson, Founder of Jaywalker Lodge and Alpha 180

Jaime Vinck: What's your why? What has driven you to this moment in time?

BF: It's a great question, and we make our clients and our staff reckon with that one too.

I think for me is that nothing matches the feeling of coming alongside another human being when the lights come on. It's everything that I think I drank and used drugs to find in the first place. A meaningful and intimate personal connection with somebody about stuff that really matters. Being with a like-minded person and having a shared experience is pinnacle for me.

In Alcoholics Anonymous, when somebody reaches deep and takes a big risk and honors me with sharing something, even a secret, as part of their step work or otherwise, I'm just so humbled by that. It lifts my spirit. It really moves me when I know people trust me personally at that level, as well as professionally with Jaywalker and Alpha 180. We are dealing with men at a critical time in their lives—that's the "why" for all of us.

JV: Sharing wasn't always natural for you, though. I find that interesting as your whole mission is to commune.

BF: Oh, yes. I was in Hazelden in Minnesota for a thirty-day program but was referred more and more and ended up there nine months. I was in a program for chronic relapsers. There were nine of us on the unit. About three months in, we had what you would call a peer evaluation group. The format was you'd go into group at eight in the morning and you'd be done at five in the afternoon, and all staff and all clients were in the group.

Essentially, we'd go around the room and assess people we had concerns about, three people at a time. So, one person could have a good one to three hours of attention in group. Much to my surprise and mortification, I was nominated as somebody needed discussion. Up to that point, I would have told you I was a leader in the group. Well, there's something wrong with that idea that you're leading in rehab, but there I was, making my bed so you could bounce a quarter off it, providing everyone else in the group with insightful feedback.

JV: And there's one in every crowd, right?

BF: I was *that* guy…I mean, I was asked to not bring a clipboard to group anymore, you know? I wanted to get everything out of this, and a gold star too! What I found out when they went around the room was there wasn't one person there that felt safe around me or felt like I was trustworthy. They said that I seemed to be aloof, arrogant, and judgmental. The group also said that I was withholding myself but was demanding of others.

I kept trying to defend myself, but the counselor would tell me to just listen and not talk. I would have my chance later. So, finally, when it came around time for my—what I considered to be—my rebuttal, I essentially chastised everyone in the room for being too cowardly to confront me personally, like "I was in the cafeteria with you yesterday, or I was on a walking path with you last week. You know you could have brought up any of this stuff, but no, you wanted to grandstand in front of the counselor like a bunch of jackals; you don't have the constitutional wherewithal to show up in your own voice." I mean, I was just brutal.

When I was done speaking, you could hear a pin drop, and nobody said anything, and my counselor turned to me and said, "You know, Bobby. The fact that nobody in this room feels comfortable enough with you to talk honestly about their feelings may not be your fault, but it's damn sure your problem—and you're going to live with this problem for the rest of your life."

That's when the walls kind of came down. Jaime, I was three months sober, and the "Bob Show" wasn't getting very good reviews. [The room was] full of people, [but] I was alone in the room, numb. There were no drugs and no alcohol. This was not a drug and alcohol problem. This was a "Bob problem." After that day, everything changed. Absolutely everything changed.

After the group said their piece and I said mine, I went to my room for about three days and the team said, "Okay, that's enough. You need to reemerge."

I remember being in group, and I started to cry. I was just blubbering on the chest of this thirty-year-old, three-hundred-pound bass player from Toledo. He had this long red hair, and he put his arm around me, and he said, "You know, don't worry, Bobby. We love you. We don't like you. But we love you."

I had never given this guy the time of day before that. I didn't even realize how much I was scanning and reading the room and putting people in their place and positioning myself all the time. All that fell away. Now, I just wanted somebody to sit next to at lunch.

All of a sudden, I was really interested in other people's suggestions about my situation. Because even though they used drugs, and we had prostituted ourselves, and we all had horror stories in our addiction, what they had was an ability to connect safely with other people. I wanted what they had. So, for the first time, I began assigning meaning to other people's comments and suggestions about my situation.

The important thing is that it happened in a peer group. It didn't happen one-on-one, so my moment of clarity was in that group—and then my other moment of clarity happened. Fast forward to what Jaywalker Lodge is today, an extended care residential treatment and recovery community for men. We're a peer-directed program, where making friends and having fun is serious business.

JV: So, in terms of Jaywalker's growth and success, and now Alpha 180, I know that you know you would use the treatment team model, and teams are very important in your work. Why do you think the team is so important?

BF: Just like the kid I was in 1992, sitting in that group all by himself, you realize we just can't do it alone. You can't even begin to counsel without building trust in a safe container. You've got to do that; it's mandatory. But the difference between a good counselor and a great counselor isn't building trust with your client. It's building trust amongst them, creating a dynamic that doesn't even involve you, because you're not leaving with them. They're leaving with each other. And that's where the magic is. We work like this organism—a soul—and we help people.

CHAPTER 4

CONSIDERING INTEGRATED TREATMENT

The Plays for Treating Co-Occurring Disorders

"Some changes look negative on the surface, but you soon realize that space is being created in your life for something new to emerge."

—ECKHART TOLLE

As a new therapist in residential treatment, my clinical supervisor would tell me to "treat the alligator closest to the boat." His advice (based on an old military expression) was to always focus on my patient's most vital and urgent issue first. Seemed like common sense. I quickly learned that oftentimes there were several alligators circling the boat, and water was pouring in. Each one of these alligators represented a potentially life-threatening problem of addiction, depression, anxiety, and trauma. How do we prioritize care and come up with a plan of attack? For example, a veteran, also a first responder, was referred for treatment after a fight at work for her post-traumatic stress disorder. In the assessment, she revealed that she also drank six to eight beers per night. Do we first confront her drinking and anger management and then begin trauma treatment, or vice versa? How about a middle-aged woman who had been misusing sleep meds for her anxiety since the onset of menopause and had made a recent suicide attempt? Do we tackle the causes of her depression and anxiety before, during, or after we have a complete hormonal workup done? These are real examples, and the answer to the questions was found in deepening my understanding of co-occurring disorders and the integrated model of care.

What Is a Co-Occurring Disorder?

Let's review some information that was mentioned earlier about co-occurring disorders. According to the Substance Abuse and Mental Health Services Administration, "the coexistence of both a mental illness and [substance use disorder] SUD is known as a co-occurring disorder and is common occurrence among people in addiction treatment." Questions frequently asked in treatment programs, are which comes first: the addiction or mental illness and do we treat disorders sequentially or simultaneously? The answer to these questions has evolved over time.

Then, according to Dr. Amanda L. Giordano in her 2021 *Psychology Today* article, which summarized the National Institution of Drug Abuse's and the National Institute of Mental Health's texts about co-occurring disorders, an "individual may turn to the gratifying properties of drugs of abuse as a way to cope with their distressing mental health symptoms.... Alcohol and other drugs are predictable, consistent methods of changing the way a person feels. If a person is in psychological distress, drugs of abuse can offer an escape, albeit temporarily. Although the use of drugs of abuse may have started as a form of 'self-medicating' psychiatric symptoms, over time, drug use exacerbates these symptoms, and can itself become another disorder, namely, a SUD." So, in this case, the mental health issue came first.

For others, chronic substance use and the negative consequences of their misuse may lead to depression, anxiety, and other mental and physical health conditions. In this situation, an individual begins using drugs and later, a mental health concern develops. Depending upon an individual's genetic makeup and biological vulnerabilities, there are also cases where the use of substances can trigger the onset of a mental illness. For example, research confirms the link between using high-potency cannabis (with higher amounts of the psychoactive ingredient, THC) with psychiatric disorders. Thus, for some individuals, the use of a drug of abuse (e.g., methamphetamine, cocaine, cannabis, synthetic drugs) can lead to the onset of mental health symptomology. In these cases, the substance use came first.

Regardless of whether the substance use or mental health issues came first, until the underlying issues are uncovered and treated, there will be a repeated pattern of treatment, recovery, and relapse. The mental health issues (most often trauma) become the fire in the basement that we have to extinguish before the metaphorical house burns down.

One of the first exercises in most treatment programs is to do a lifeline, telling your life story and highlighting significant events both good and bad. I was trained to listen for the wounding, the painful events that started that fire in the basement. These wounds can be directly linked to patterns of use and when discussed, create moments of understanding and validation for patients. Many patients have been masking and minimizing their pain for so long. Finding that they have nothing to be ashamed of and they have more in common than different from the other group members (and therapists) present is a powerful and cathartic experience.

It is all too common for people seeking treatment to resist a mental health diagnosis, preferring to think of their substance use as an allergy. I had a client who used to joke, "Whenever I drink, I break out in handcuffs." He would not, however, look at the role that his symptoms of bipolar disorder played in his pattern of use. Part of this, I believe, is that the stigma around mental health remains all too real. The same applies to mental health patients. They will often deny substance use and resist working on their unhealthy relationships with alcohol or drugs at all costs. The stigma on both sides is real, and the professional ramifications of losing the ability to make a living if one has either diagnosis often fuels the denial.

The truth of the matter is that co-occurring disorders are on the rise, and they affect and are affected by one another.

It is also important to consider the physical dimension to a co-occurring disorder. We are physical, emotional, and spiritual beings. Our physical symptoms influence our emotions. Our emotions bring on physical symptoms. It is impossible to separate these coexisting conditions as they influence each other.

Choosing a treatment center that can meet your needs from all perspectives is critical to your success, and there is plenty of evidence to support what components are to be part of the treatment model. Raising your awareness of the mind, body, spirit connection as you seek treatment is critical. I chose to discuss it in this chapter specifically because neglecting one of the major areas, can contribute to the cycle of relapse. I am not suggesting that any one treatment center has the capability to "fix" your mind, body, and spirit. I am saying that a good program will begin the process of understanding where the emotional and physical pain points exist and work with you to create a comprehensive roadmap to address them throughout the continuum of care.

"Raising your awareness of the mind, body, spirit connection as you seek treatment is critical."

Before we dive into the evidenced-based recommended model of treatment for co-occurring disorders, we will focus on what is going on for you right now—mind, body, and spirit.

Play 1. Activate and Nurture the Mind, Body, Spirit Connection

Right now, as you read this book and explore more about the journey you are taking toward treatment, you might feel a physical tension in your neck or your back. Your energy level may be low, and your mind rambling unkind thoughts in your head. Addiction affects all parts of the self—our minds, our physical bodies, and our sense of purpose. The power of what we feel in our minds, our bodies, and our spirit is very real, and there is no greater time to learn how the integration of all of the elements of yourself can support the literal integration of treatment for co-occurring disorders.

Here's how each element plays a role in treatment, especially when it comes to co-occurring disorders:

Mind: This helps you understand your wounds throughout your life and the ways that you have coped with them, both healthy and unhealthy. Specifically, look at unresolved grief, trauma (adverse childhood experiences), and symptoms of depression and anxiety.

Body: A history and physical are key components of a residential treatment program, including full blood work. Also, a pain assessment and pain scale are done frequently throughout your stay. Not only is substance use hard on your body, but there may be underlying factors that contribute to use that could be uncovered. You will also learn things, such as where anger and anxiety show up in your body, which can be helpful in behavioral changes.

Spirit: This means different things to different people. The 12-step program teaches us to believe in a power greater than ourselves as step one. For some, it's a sense of purpose in finding passion in helping others. For others, it's a reconnection to faith. I think of it as you feeding your soul. Making meaning of one's life becomes a fundamental part of the treatment and recovery journey.

Work It!

Think about where you are today—mind, body, and spirit. Take a moment and write down brief answers. After you have read your answers, imagine what you would like your life to look like in each category. Visualize it and then write down what the future life would look like:

Mind:

Body:

Spirit:

Play 2. Understand Integrated Approaches

The Substance Abuse and Mental Health Services Administration (SAMHSA) recommends an integrated treatment approach for treating co-occurring disorders. Integrated treatment involves treating the symptoms simultaneously (or braided treatment) rather than treating each disorder separately or sequentially without consideration for the other. There was a time in treatment where a patient could not work on their mental health issues until they had been sober for a number of months and that the SUD providers did not coordinate care with the mental health providers

Evidence shows that an integrated treatment model of care offers the most hope for the effective treatment of co-occurring disorders. An integrated treatment model treats the substance use disorder and co-occurring disorder(s), both mental and physical, simultaneously. It involves a collaborative, team approach, utilizing the expertise of various specialties to coordinate patients' treatment plans.

With an integrated model of treatment, no disorder is identified as being "primary" or "underlying" in relation to another disorder. Instead, all co-occurring disorders are treated as one unit that is causing dysfunction and despair in your life.

According to [source], the benefits of an of an integrated model of care

- reaffirm the relationship of a practitioner and patient through a team
- focus on whole person
- is informed by evidence; and
- make use of appropriate therapeutic approaches and disciplines to optimize health and healing.

Other benefits of this model of care include the following:

- Addresses physical, emotional and spiritual aspects of life
- Non-hierarchical
- Focuses on prevention and education
- Takes a holistic approach
- Includes social supports

An integrated model of care is relationship centric. The practitioner and the patient are working together, and their relationship becomes as important as any procedure, laboratory test, or pill. This is accomplished through a team of professionals who collaborate on behalf of the patient. The goal of the team is to deliver comprehensive psychosocial treatment that is evidence based and personally tailored to allow for personal definitions of recovery. The team will meet several times a week to discuss each patient's progress on their treatment goals.

When searching for treatment, it is important to ensure that all of the major categories described above exist in the program of choice. In our "Meet Your Teammates" chapter (chapter 6), you will be provided with a description of each team member's role, as well as questions to ask them in your search for the right program. We will also review the recommended evidence-based treatment modalities to use in your search. Having a massage therapist and a pony does not make a program integrated!

For Fans and Family

What's the difference between integrative and integrated?

> *Integrated treatment* treats substance use disorder and mental health simultaneously and treats the whole person with evidence-based practices.
>
> *Integrative treatment* includes the most well-researched, conventional medicine with the most well-researched, evidence-based complementary (previously known as alternative) therapies. Common complementary practices in treatment centers include acupuncture, massage, yoga, music, and equine therapy.

Research shows that outcomes for both substance use and mental health disorders are improved, including fewer relapses, when family members are actively involved in the treatment process. However, the experience of living with and trying to care for family members or friends who struggle with addiction is traumatic, and each family member must have their own space to heal from the situation. When each family member invests in their own healing, the entire unit is better prepared for the long recovery road ahead. Put on your own oxygen mask before helping others. (The "oxygen" components will be discussed in the "Family Communication" chapter.)

Circle of Support

There were eight students in my post-graduate intensive on treating trauma. We were asked by our professor to tell our life stories in linear fashion from birth to present day. In this particular exercise(we were asked to create our own trauma narrative, where we would focus on main areas of the most painful events of our lives and share how these events had shaped us personally and professionally.

We heard heart-wrenching stories of abandonment and loss, and the wisdom gained from the pain experienced. When it was her turn, one student stood and presented her story. When she was fifteen, she ran for student body president and lost to her archrival. She had misused drugs and suffered with disordered eating for years after this particular wound. The room was silent. She teared up. One particularly angry student said, "That's it? You lost an election, and I got orphaned at birth when my parents overdosed? How dare you!"

Our brilliant instructor looked at the angry student and said, "How dare *you*. Everyone's pain is maximum to them."

We were all moved to tears by the lesson in empathy, which I know I have never forgotten.

Play 3. Acknowledge Adverse Childhood Experiences

A 1995 Study conducted by the Centers for Disease Control and Kaiser Permanente healthcare organization revealed that those individuals who experienced an adverse childhood experience were more likely to have certain mental and physical ailments later in life. Examples of these experiences are abuse, neglect, and household dysfunction that creates an environment of toxic stress for the child that may negatively impact their entire life.

If you have concerns or curiosity about your childhood trauma, the Adverse Childhood Experience self-screening tool is available on line through a variety of sources. (www.aceaware.org). Completing the ACE screening and having this information when making your decision for treatment provides you with more information on availability of specialized treatments. Specifically, if you have a high ACE score, ensure that your center of choice is trauma informed and that the therapists are properly trained and credentialed. We will talk more about this in the chapter titled, "The Treatment Components and Daily Schedule."

CHAPTER 5

FINANCIAL FACTS AND IMPACTS

The Plays for Paying for Treatment

"The first wealth is health."

—RALPH WALDO EMERSON

Early in my practice, the typical trajectory for someone seeking treatment was to go to detox, then thirty-plus days in residential, followed by an "aftercare" plan that included a support group (usually 12-step) and possibly one-on-one counseling. This approach to substance use disorder (SUD) treatment was largely based on acute care models that focused on reducing symptoms, clinical stabilization, and subsequent discharge. These were single, unlinked treatment episodes followed by brief "aftercare" services, upon which treatment relationships end and the person was expected to achieve long-term recovery on their own. I recall as a primary therapist in a residential treatment program, before outpatient programs were readily available, having to sever my relationship with my patient. We were not allowed to work with patients after they were discharged from residential for a variety of reasons—some financial, some philosophical, and some downright punitive.

The acute model of care proved unable to address the needs of people in recovery from severe and chronic SUD, who sometimes go through several episodes of care (cycle of remission, relapse, and repeat treatment) before achieving sustained recovery. These patients were often labeled "chronic relapsers" and commonly not allowed to return to their treatment centers for care after relapse. When a chronic relapser would come into care, there would be flags to alert staff that they may be "gamey" or other shaming terms. (Imagine, someone being denied entry into a hospital because they had another heart attack or their cancer came back or being labeled as "difficult" because of their return to care.)

Along with the shift from viewing SUD in an acute model to chronic model of care, there was a significant change in the law that allowed people to use their insurance to pay for SUD treatment. The 2008 Mental Health Parity and Addiction Equity Act (MHPAEA) and the 2010 Affordable Care Act (ACA) expanded access to behavioral health services. Together, these policies expanded access to behavioral health treatment to an estimated 62.5 million individuals. The ACA was a game changer in addiction treatment and allowed us to truly expand access to care. (Prior to the Mental Health Parity Act, insurers were not required to cover mental health diagnoses.)

The ACA increased treatment options and extends many benefits of employer-provided insurance plans to individual medical insurance plans. The ACA also allowed adults twenty six and younger to remain on their parents' healthcare plan and receive much needed care. The other interesting component is that the ACA added substance use disorders as one of the ten elements of essential health benefits. This meant that all health insurance sold on health insurance exchanges or provided by Medicaid were mandated to include services for substance use disorders. Hurrah!

Because this expanded insurance reimbursement was a reality, outpatient programs were popping up across the country. I was involved in opening one such intensive outpatient program in 2010, where we provided care to patients from two different care pathways: one as a step-down from residential and one as a direct admission to outpatient services. Little did I know that I was part of a groundbreaking national movement to expand access to care through outpatient services that continues today.

I recall that from a licensure standpoint, many states did not have the licensing requirements in place to adequately regulate the number of programs and new levels of care that were being launched.

The outpatient program I was launching was part of a residential program, and for the first time, upon graduation, our patients could "step down" to continue their care. This option was extremely well received among our patients, as they could continue their work with the same staff and program components as their residential treatment. Also, if someone was not able to attend residential or if they did not require residential from a clinical or medical standpoint, they could join our outpatient program.

The number of outpatient options has only expanded, with many virtual programs being opened during COVID-19. This has been a positive occurrence, with more points of entry available and more openness on the part of treatment providers to demonstrate flexibility when it comes to how and when someone enters care. Still, there is a lot of work to be done in making quality care more assessable and affordable.

Paying for addiction treatment has contributed to the financial ruin of many families, and sadly, they don't always get their desired outcome. I believe that lack of access to quality care can be attributed, at least in part, to the complexity of paying for treatment. For example, many folks with insurance don't realize that their loved ones are covered under their polices, or there is no time or willingness to sit on the phone with the insurance carrier to find out what is covered—all before the whole process of selecting treatment. Keep in mind that most often the investigative work is done by loved ones who are drained both emotionally and financially by the situation. Treatment options range from state and federally funded programs with zero out of pocket to self-pay luxury programs that cost at least $100,000 per month. Most individuals fit somewhere in between. People are desperate to get their loved ones the care that they deserve. Unfortunately, there are unscrupulous players in the industry that attempt to take advantage of families when they are most vulnerable. This is done in a variety of ways, including misrepresenting what their program has to offer, over

"While treatment for an addiction can be costly, it is also an important investment in your health, your life, and your future, and one that will likely pay you back for years to come."

charging, and encouraging treatment that is beyond your financial means.

Please take comfort in knowing that regardless of your financial situation, there is a program for you. While treatment for an addiction can be costly, it is also an important investment in your health, your life, and your future, and one that will likely pay you back for years to come. Knowing the right questions to ask, avoiding unethical players, and getting the program that you can *afford* across the continuum of care are the key plays in this section of the playbook.

Play 1. Weigh Your Options for Treatment Payment

Far too many people avoid getting the treatment they need and deserve because of a fear of the financial implications. There is also a learning curve as you or someone you trust begins to consider all the elements and benefits or downsides to a certain payment path. I have seen people with insurance decide to self-pay because of restrictions, co-pays, or denial of coverage, while others have found state-funded treatment centers to be appropriate for their lifestyles and family location. There is no right or wrong here. But patience and self-care during this process will help you retrieve the information necessary to make payment decisions.

Treatment is paid for via the following options:

- Self-pay
- Insurance
- State-funded programs

- Medicare
- Financing

Self-Pay

Self-pay is when you choose to pay for rehabilitation out of pocket, rather than by using insurance or other sources. This can be a viable pathway when you don't have insurance coverage or for privacy reasons.

People choose self-pay when they find the benefits suited to them. These benefits include flexibility and choice, beyond the limited facilities that might be in-network with their insurance provider. With the self-pay option, people choose a program that meets their needs and preferences. Other benefits of self-pay are privacy and confidentiality (you can avoid having SUD treatment show up as part of the history on the medical records) and immediate access to care. Individuals can often start treatment more quickly when paying out of pocket, as they don't need to wait for insurance approval or navigate bureaucratic hurdles.

The downsides of self-pay can be higher out-of-pocket costs, as you are responsible for the full cost of treatment. Depending on type and duration, this cost can be devastating. When you are not protected by insurance coverage, you may be responsible for any unexpected costs or complications that might occur while receiving treatment.

It is also important to understand that if you are self-paying and are insured, you may be entitled to an out-of-network benefit, meaning that if you are concerned about limited choices and want to expand your search for rehab programs, you will be able to consider a center not in the insurer's network partially covered by the provider with a percentage shared by you. Your chosen center may or may not handle the claim submission for you to receive a partial reimbursement. An important point, when tallying up the self-pay costs, is to not forget to factor in step-down treatments, especially if you are choosing to go to residential treatment. Gather the costs of intensive outpatient programs and partial hospitalization programs so you can get a sense of the entire financial picture. Be aware of the "à la carte" services. You may be quoted an all-inclusive rate per day or for a given time period (often thirty days). Please be sure to ask what is included in the rate. Incidental services such as massages, naturopathic medicine, personal training, and so on may be added to your daily rate. Understanding what is included prevents disappointment and potentially triggering situations when you or your loved one are in treatment.

Insurance

My passion for the past several years has been to expand access to high-quality, high-value treatment, meaning treatment that can be provided by using one's insurance. Many of us pay a lot of money in insurance premiums, and the fact that there are limited options for folks that are insurance dependent has kept me up many a night. In my work while speaking with large groups of employees across industries, it's clear to me that employees don't understand their mental health benefit coverage.

To make matters worse, there is a lack of understanding that family members covered under their policy are also eligible for mental health services. Insurance coverage for addiction treatment varies depending on your plan and other factors. Insurance can be employer sponsored, independently purchased, or purchased on the healthcare exchange through the ACA. Aside from the unexpected costs, people are usually blindsided by bills they didn't know they'd be responsible for. This is because when seeking insurance benefits to cover the cost of treatment, people don't have an accurate understanding of what their responsibility will be. Insurance details are often not explicit, so it's important to exercise patience and foresee every possible scenario and ask questions. More details are usually available on insurance websites, where you can take your time reading through and possibly reread. Ask others who you trust for help and guidance. Perhaps your behavioral health professional can offer strategies or worst-case scenarios. Preparedness is key. Nobody wants to open the mailbox and find a bill for thousands of dollars you have no idea how to pay for.

My best advice when taking the insurance route is to get the care you need, maximizing use of your insurance benefits, and have a plan for other components. Far too many people, out of urgency, take on the opposite mindset: get the care I need and figure out how to pay for it later.

Don't assume your treatment program of choice will file claims for you. And when centers do submit the claim on your behalf, ask them if they keep a percentage of the reimbursement. Depending on the insurance company, payments may go directly to the rehab center, or a check is cut to you and you will then pay the treatment center. Most treatment centers expect payment up front, and you keep the reimbursement. Knowing where the money is going and how it is being distributed saves a lot of guess work and mistakes. Regardless of who submits the claim for reimbursement, it is important to understand where the reimbursement check will be sent. If it is going to you or your loved one, having a plan in place to receive the money and make appropriate arrangements for it is key. We have seen many recovery journeys derailed because someone gets a check in the mail without any notice or accountability. Again, please be sure that there are funds available for your step-down (partial hospitalization program, intensive outpatient program) care.

Work It!

Take a deep breath. Place both feet on the floor and ground yourself. When it comes to embarking on the insurance process, remember: you got this.

Review your insurance plan benefits and coverage by taking the following steps:

- Pull out the insurance card and familiarize yourself with the information on it.
- Look on your health insurance plan website or call your insurer to obtain a summary of benefits and coverage for mental health and addiction treatment. As you review your summary of benefits and coverage, talk with a representative and ask these questions:
    - What mental health/SUD services does my plan cover?
    - Are healthcare providers required to get prior authorization from the insurance company before treating SUDs?

- What, if any, out-of-pocket expenses (deductibles or co-pays) are there? How are they estimated?
- Are there limits on the number of days or episodes of treatment that are covered?
- Which treatment providers are in my insurance network? (Choosing from this list can help prevent unexpected costs.)
- Do I also have out-of-network benefits?

- It can take many calls to figure this information out, and the conversation may be difficult. You can ask a trusted person for help. You may consider allowing your trusted person to make the calls for you. Ask your health insurance provider to help you authorize someone to speak about your coverage and care.

Once you speak with the insurance company, confirm details by speaking with the treatment center.

- Verify that the treatment center is in network with the insurance company.
- Ask the treatment center about your payment responsibilities and when payment is due. This will likely include meeting a deductible, patient share, and/or co-payment.

Patient share refers to the portion of healthcare costs that you, as the patient, are responsible for paying out of your own pocket. It includes various types of cost-sharing arrangements covered by your health insurance plan.

Here are the common forms of patient share:

1. **Deductible:**
   - The deductible is the amount you must pay for certain services before your health plan starts covering your expenses.
   - It typically applies once per calendar year and can vary significantly in size.
   - Unlike coinsurance (which is a percentage of the bill), the deductible is a pre-determined fixed amount.
2. **Coinsurance:**
   - Coinsurance is the percentage of the total cost of a covered service that you share with your insurance provider after meeting your deductible.
   - For example, if your coinsurance rate is 20 percent, you pay 20 percent of the bill and your insurance covers the remaining 80 percent.
3. **Co-payment (Co-pay):**
   - A co-payment is a fixed amount you pay for specific healthcare services after meeting your deductible.
   - Unlike coinsurance, co-pays apply to individual services (examples include doctor visits or prescription drugs).

The National Association of Addiction Treatment Providers' *The Addiction Treatment Provider Quality Assurance Guidebook, A Guide to the Core Competencies for the Delivery of Addiction Treatment Services* (2nd ed.) provides us with guidance on the ethical practices in the handling of patient share. "Addiction treatment providers should, by policy, collect all patient responsibility under the insurance policy being billed including deductibles and copayments, in alignment with the network contract, or policy documents when billing out of network. Exceptions to the policy should be documented, comply with insurance policy or contract guidelines, and not be standard business practice. Routine waiver of patient financial responsibility related to deductibles and co-pays is prohibited. Waivers must not be provided except in the case of demonstrable financial hardship, based on written objective criteria in alignment with insurance policy guidelines."

If the treatment center is going to pay for your transportation, waive patient share, or provide you with a discount rate or scholarship, they may ask you to complete paperwork demonstrating financial need. This ensures that they are operating in an ethical and legal manner and should not be a cause for alarm.

- Factors may differ depending on the care setting for addiction treatment, such as outpatient or residential care, so be sure to ask for specifics. Please note that in January if you have not met your deductible, your contribution or patient share will be higher.
- Make sure the insurance plan covers medications for addiction treatment if you're being treated for opioid use disorder.
- Understand if the rehab is going to get a pre-authorization for your care and how they handle concurrent reviews for additional time.
- If you are denied coverage for care, ask if the treatment center will appeal and what member of your treatment

team will argue on your behalf for staying in care. If you are denied again, ask them to appeal again. You can also advocate for yourself by calling the insurance company. Your insurance company is required to provide you with the standards they used to deny care. They may say it was deemed "not medically necessary," in which case, ask your medical provider to provide information on medical necessity.

- If you are traveling for treatment, ask the rehab if you are responsible for purchasing your own transportation (flight, car rental, and so on).

After you are admitted to treatment:

- Keep any documentation of communication with your insurance plan. This includes explanation of benefits, phone calls, emails, bills, and/or denial letters.
- Ask them to keep you or the financially responsible party in the loop on authorizations and insurance process.
- If you receive a surprise bill for care, reach out to the business office of your treatment center immediately.

State-Funded Programs

State-funded rehab is funded by state governments and typically provide access to addiction treatment for those not able to afford private rehab or who do not have insurance coverage. State-funded rehab programs can offer a variety of services, with little to no out-of-pocket expense, from detoxification and inpatient/residential treatment to outpatient treatment and medication-assisted treatment. This involves using medications, such as methadone or buprenorphine, to facilitate long-term recovery. Eligibility may be considered based on income, where you reside (such as which state), and level or severity of addiction. State-funded programs are notorious for having waiting lists or limited availability. There are more options at the outpatient level of care. They also might not offer your desired amenities or individualized care as compared to private rehabilitation treatment.

You can also find state-funded programs through Medicaid, nonprofits, hospitals, and community centers.

Medicaid

Under the ACA, behavioral health services became mandatory for public insurance (Medicaid) to cover in every state. As an "essential health"

For Fans and Family

It isn't uncommon for the search for funding to be spearheaded by a friend or family member. You might be considered by the rehab program and/or the insurance provider, the financially responsible party (FRP). What does this mean?

When it comes to rehab treatment, an FRP is the person or entity paying for the costs of treatment. The FRP may be the patient themselves, a family member, friend, an insurance company, or a government agency. Typically, during the admissions process, the FRP is determined and may be required to sign financial agreements or provide proof of insurance coverage. In the case of financing offered through a rehab center, the FRP will be the one applying. As the FRP, you may be responsible for a range of costs, so it is important to communicate with the person seeking treatment what you will and will not help pay for, so everyone's roles are clear.

Paying for treatment or being the FRP does mean that you have access to information about treatment beyond financial matters. Your loved one will need to sign a release of information for you to be able to speak with their treatment providers. If you are paying for treatment, share your expectations on communication *before* your loved one starts the process. This will reduce the risk of resentments and misunderstandings on the sharing of information.

benefit, addiction treatment cannot be denied to a patient under public insurance. Some programs take both in-network insurance benefits and Medicaid policies.

If you are below a certain household income threshold, you may qualify for Medicaid. If you or a loved one are pregnant and/or are below nineteen years of age, you automatically qualify for Medicaid.

For Medicaid information, find your state and then search for benefits and coverage. Review your summary of benefits and coverage, or ask a representative.

Community health centers

Community health centers or a hospital or state-run medical facility may be another option. Community health centers are nonprofit health providers that may be able to assist with treatment costs or offer an option for payment based on what you are able to pay at the time. The intake department or social worker at the community mental health agency can provide you with more information on a sliding scale.

Nonprofit programs

Programs like The Salvation Army and 10,000 Beds offer no-cost treatment options for drug and alcohol. Both offer residential options with eligibility based on availability.

Medicare

Finally, the last payment option is Medicare, a federal health insurance program for people over sixty-five. Medicare will cover most of the following treatment costs:

- Outpatient mental health treatment
- Inpatient mental health treatment (staying overnight for treatment)
- Opioid use treatment
- Tobacco use treatment
- Alcohol misuse counseling

If you get Medicare benefits through a supplement like one of the Medicare Advantage plans (like a health maintenance organization, or HMO, or preferred provider organization, or PPO) or other Medicare health plan, check your plan's website, materials, or call the number on the back of your Medicare card.

If you get your Medicare benefits through traditional Medicare (not a Medicare Advantage plan) and want more information, visit Medicare.gov.

Financing

If private funding is out of the question or if you are unable to cover the costs of patient share, some treatment facilities may offer financing plans that allow you to make payments after discharge. This arrangement is sometimes offered through a third-party lender that can create a loan package. Be sure to discuss financing options with any treatment center being considered. Be aware that many of these financing companies charge very high interest rates.

Often in treatment, there will be well-intentioned patients who are well resourced and offer to pay for their peers' treatment. I have also seen several patients chip in to cover the treatment costs of someone in their group. I don't recommend this practice, and most treatment centers frown on it because it often creates drama, as well as rescuing and victim behavior on the part of the patients. We will discuss the drama triangle in the Chapter 8 on Family Matters.

Treatment centers have also been known to provide scholarships to potential patients. This isn't a common practice. However, if you find that you have no other option, then it's worth asking. I have seen scholarships given most frequently when someone does not have the funds to continue treatment, for whatever reason, and their team believes they need more care.

Play 2. Put Cost into Perspective

Millions of people affected by drugs and alcohol continue to endure the damages of addiction because they don't think they can afford to get help. Looking honestly at the cost of your addiction may change your mind. Whether you or your loved one uses drugs, see where drugs and alcohol damage your finances by doing this exercise.

Go to a quiet, safe place with a pen and paper. Breathe deeply. Get real with yourself by having your bank/credit/debit card statements handy, and write down the answers to the following questions:

1. How much have you spent on your drug of choice in the past year?

2. If you are a smoker, how much have you spent on cigarettes?
3. How much have you spent on Ubers because you were too drunk to drive? (You've made a good choice—but it can add up.)
4. What objects have you needed to repair or replace this month because of drug- or alcohol-related accidents?
5. How many times have you needed to go to the hospital for a drug- or alcohol-related injury?
6. What did you have to pay in fees for co-pay?
7. Has your insurance premium gone up?
8. Has drugs or alcohol worsened an illness you have, such as heart disease or depression?
9. How much are you spending on prescriptions, medical devices, or other medical services because of worsened symptoms?
10. How much time do you miss at work because of drugs or alcohol?
11. How much has this cost you hourly?
12. How much has this cost you in bonuses, promotions, or pay raises?
13. What services do you use because drugs or alcohol make you unable to complete tasks? (Dining out, child services, cleaning, and so on.) How much did you spend on these services this week?
14. Have you overspent while shopping, dining out, or otherwise because you were intoxicated? How much did you overspend this week?

15. What legal issues have you had because of behavior on drugs or alcohol? What fees did you have to pay a lawyer, for a bond, or in reparations?

Tally up the cost of your addiction. Are you surprised? In relation to what a rehab treatment might cost, can you see that you are already spending money at not only a financial cost to you but also at an emotional cost to you and those who love you.

Circle of Support

Very early in the launch of our outpatient program, I was doing all the assessments for admission in collaboration with our medical director. One day a well-dressed man, we will call him Jack, in his early forties came in for an assessment. Jack explained that while he was a very highly functioning executive, his use of recreational drugs had increased, and he was destroying his career and marriage. Jack was scared.

Jack also shared that if he took time from work for residential treatment, he would be fired. Making matters worse was if he got fired, his wife would leave him. Their marriage was hanging on by a thread, and if he lost the ability to provide for his family, it would be over. Jack and his wife had a young daughter, and she was the center of his universe. The idea of not living with his daughter on a day-to-day basis was more than he could bear. Jack had a plan. He had thoroughly researched our new outpatient program, and he wanted to enroll. My immediate thought was "Hell no, you need residential." But Jack begged me to give him a shot and promised that if he could not stay sober while in outpatient, he would immediately check in to residential and suffer the consequences.

This was new territory for me as well, so I quickly got our medical director on board to evaluate any health risk and to get his support in creating an outpatient treatment plan. Jack was our first intensive outpatient program patient that had not completed our residential treatment program. He was not "stepping down" in care. The intensive outpatient program was where his care plan began. We were able to create wrap-around services that provided much of the support that he would have received in residential. This included attending our intensive outpatient program (group and one-on-one therapy) nine hours per week for three months, medication management with our physician, marriage counseling, and intensive 12-step work with a sponsor.

Jack hit the ground running and became a leader in our program. He successfully completed his outpatient program and continued one-on-one counseling with me for the next five years. I can tell you that while there have been some bumps in the road, Jack is sober, still married, and his daughter is about to graduate from high school. By sharing his story without stigma or shame, Jack makes it possible for other employees at his company to go to treatment when needed. He also hires newly sober folks in his business, not only providing jobs but career paths for people in recovery.

I am sure that there are thousands of stories like Jack's: people who were able to get help because of the ACA, the commitment on the part of businesses to take a chance on new levels of care, and the willingness of clinicians to experience a paradigm shift by demonstrating flexibility in the care pathway.

Play 3. Know Your Rights at Your Workplace

If you are employed full time, you may qualify for the Family and Medical Leave Act. The Family and Medical Leave Act is a federal law that was passed by President Bill Clinton in 1993. The law was a game changer for working families as it provided job protection and health care for 12 weeks for certain medical and family reasons.

For the first time, employees seeking addiction treatment were protected from job loss under the FMLA. FMLA also ensures that you won't be mistreated or demoted because you are in treatment. You will, however, be required to provide documentation of your disorder and treatment to your human resources department. In addition, your employer may offer short-term disability benefits. Depending on your plan, you may receive between 50 to 60 percent of your salary while on disability.

Before you go to treatment, please understand what your eligibility and benefits are under both of these programs. Your treatment center provider has responsibility for completing the paperwork to secure these benefits. Candidly, some centers do a great job, while others do a poor job and jeopardize benefits. Please be sure that you are comfortable with the center's knowledge and ability to complete the paperwork in a timely manner. Knowing that these steps have been taken will provide you, and your loved ones, a great deal of comfort.

CHAPTER 6

MEET YOUR TEAMMATES

The Plays for Maximizing the Expertise of Your Treatment Professionals

"Alone we can do so little. Together, we can do so much."

—HELEN KELLER

Here you are. The action stage is in full swing as you determine the level of care appropriate for you, solicit the guidance of healthcare professionals and other trusted sources, and explore the financial options available to you. It's time to meet the professionals. In the introduction, I gave a proud shout-out to my fellow colleagues in the recovery field, because most of them are dedicated to helping people realize their goals of living a life in recovery from a substance use disorder. These professionals run the gamut from those who have studied long and hard, gone to medical school, or other professional training to the loyal staff who make things run and who are eager to raise the quality of living for those in residential treatment.

Regardless of whether you are in residential treatment or are in one of the types of outpatient care, a successful treatment outcome is dependent on the knowledge, skills, and ability of the key players involved in care delivery. Collaboration between these team members is essential, and the energy of the team creates—or fails to create—the soul of a treatment program. The programs are only as good as the people who work in them. When seeking treatment, understanding the roles of these important people, how they are selected, and the credentials that they hold is essential for two reasons. First, we need to ensure that the folks working in the centers are qualified to deliver the treatments that they promise. For example, if we are looking for trauma treatment and we have heard good things about eye movement desensitization and reprocessing, we want to be sure that there is a therapist that has the appropriate certification. Second, we need to ensure that the programs have staff who have the minimum qualifications to deliver the services we need. For example, if we know that we want medication-assisted treatment, the qualifications and ability of the medical provider on staff who would prescribe this treatment becomes essential. Equipping you to utilize the information in the following pages as your own tool is the goal of this chapter.

Quality programs have quality players working in them—from the kitchen staff to the CEO. Ensuring that you have the right positions and players on your team is an essential part of the treatment journey. In order to pick your team, there are key positions that are important to understand. There are some positions that are obvious, like your therapist or your medical provider. It is recommended to work with a team that takes a trauma-informed approach to treatment. This means that they recognize that the emotional wounds suffered in childhood and beyond result in the creation of coping mechanisms needed for survival. If your team doesn't understand or take the time to provide this level of insight, it may be time to change teams.

There are also roles that are not seemingly as important; however, as you will see, the folks in these positions can have a profound impact on a treatment experience. There are also leadership positions that we will discuss, like CEO, founder, or executive director, that set the tone and culture for the program.

Many of us who work in treatment are wounded healers, identifying more with patients than the rest of the world. We want to pay back some of the grace the world has shown us. Those who approach it with patience, compassion, and humor, day in and out, year after year, are nothing short of heroic.

> ***"If your team doesn't understand or take the time to provide this level of insight, it may be time to change teams."***

The team becomes a family in service of the patient. When someone is hurt, we rally around them. When someone leaves treatment, either for happy or sad reasons, there is a palpable energetic shift throughout this newly created family. This is true in a treatment center when employees move on, when a patient completes or leaves treatment, and even when an animal who is part of the treatment family passes away.

Each team member/role description is followed by a series of suggested questions to ask when you are researching treatment options. Most of the questions, as you will see, focus on credentials, turnover, licensing, and staffing practices. As we have discussed, many treatment programs hire folks that are new in recovery and often their own alumni. Some programs require staff to have two years in sustained recovery (for frontline positions) others will hire someone with one year. I recommend asking what the policy is for frontline positions. Best practice is at least one year; I prefer two years, especially for frontline positions.

Regardless of whether you are looking for your own treatment or looking for a loved one, these plays will apply to you. Although most the team members are geared toward residential treatment, there is much to learn from reading about the roles and recommended questions when pursuing outpatient treatment as well. Even if you have committed to a program or have limited options for treatment, having this information will assist you in creating an individualized treatment plan and quality experience for yourself or your loved one by making you a more informed consumer.

Play 1. Meet the People Behind the Scenes

Role: The Founder

Founders are serial entrepreneurs with heart. Able to repeatedly create successful businesses from creative ideas, these special individuals do it with compassion and empathy. Often in recovery themselves, they utilize their time, talent, and experience to provide others with the gift of recovery. Many founders invest their entire life savings, take out high-interest loans, or borrow money from family and friends to open their facilities. If they fail, they risk financial devastation. They also put their relationships with family, and even their own recovery, at risk.

Founders hold tremendous power over their patients and staff, power capable of going to their heads, especially if they are in early recovery and have not done enough of their own work. Founders are frequently on site at their programs, making themselves available to patients and families. Some founders, motivated by sharing their experiences and paying their recovery forward, become visionaries and industry leaders. Others fall in love with this new version of themselves, become obsessed with power, and get lost in the illusion of control.

If you have seen the movie *Body Brokers*, you understand the immeasurable damage unscrupulous founders inflict upon struggling families and the rehab industry. Released in February of 2021, the movie addresses the issue of "patient brokering," a fraudulent way of admitting clients into rehab centers. One mom, Alice, whose son got involved in the vicious cycle of patient brokering, wrote in the Partnership to End Addiction blog:

> With the growing number of drug treatment facilities, many unscrupulous players in the treatment industry are participating in kickback schemes known as patient brokering or "body brokering." In return for referring a patient to a drug treatment facility, the broker receives a generous compensation of $500 to $5,000. Brokers will offer to share these kickbacks with patients or entice them with substances to leave an existing facility and

> qualify for another because they have relapsed. These brokers troll AA meetings, coffee shops in popular rehab towns and, in my son's case, detox and rehab facilities.

Fortunately, through the hard work of the Department of Justice and supporting organizations, the bad actors have paid the high price of huge fines and jail time. The past decade has created opportunities for founders to sell their programs for tens of millions of dollars. It is now rare to find a founder/owner still running their own programs. When you do find one, it is a rare gift. They set the tone, culture, and values for the rehab facility. They are the spiritual center of the program and the keeper of sacred traditions.

For Fans and Family

Patient brokering is an illegal practice that has become an increasing concern in the recovery industry. It is when patients are "recruited" and referred to treatment providers in exchange for kickbacks or other forms of compensation. Some treatment centers have been caught paying exorbitant amounts of money to third-party "recruiters" who bring them new patients. Because the focus is on financial incentives, the priority is not patient care but profits. Sometimes patient brokering refers a person to a program that is not appropriate for their needs.

Patient brokers are paid by the treatment programs to seek out patients whose insurance will cover drug testing and other services. Another tactic of patient brokers is to enroll potential patients into an insurance plan with bogus addresses, pay the premiums, and then refer them to specific facilities to receive a commission. Another tactic used by sober halfway houses and treatment centers is to lure patients in by offering free cigarettes, prepaid debit cards, or other incentives. Another despicable tactic is to have someone go to a sober-living house, facilitate a relapse, and then send them back to treatment.

The best defense against patient brokering is a good offense. Ensure that the facility is reputable by going back to the basics such as state licensure, Joint Commission, or Commission on Accreditation of Rehabilitation Facilities (usually mentioned as CARF) accreditation and its listing on the Substance Abuse and Mental Health Services Administration website.

Role: CEO/Executive Director

The ultimate responsibility of running a treatment center lies with the CEO/executive director. A CEO oversees multiple operations, from planning growth initiatives to delivering high-quality care. The CEO sets goals, manages finances and budgets, hires and manages staff, creates policies and procedures, builds relationships with other community organizations and healthcare professionals, and monitors patient outcomes.

CEOs can have a clinical or non-clinical background, however, having their own "why" to guide, motivate, and keep them attached to the mission of providing quality treatment is essential. When CEOs (myself included) drift too far from their purpose, it can have a negative impact on the quality of care. Like the founder, a good CEO/executive director works at the treatment center and is accessible to their team, patients, and visiting family members.

The role of CEO is not for the faint of heart. The CEO/executive director must have the courage to make tough decisions while remaining calm in the face of great stress, tragedy, or the unknown. COVID-19 is a perfect example.

The COVID-19 pandemic placed CEOs in precarious positions as they strove to keep the doors open for struggling patients while maintaining the safety of team members and their families. Due to the allotment of government funds (Paycheck Protection Program loans), many treatment centers survived. The strain of the pandemic took an incredible toll on CEOs, with patients delaying treatment because of COVID-19 exposure, and the high prices of things needed to stay afloat (personal protective equipment, COVID-19 tests, and so on). Some CEOs could pivot and start up virtual outpatient platforms to keep the doors open and staff employed; however, it was grueling, and many suffered from extreme burnout. Some stepped out of the field all together.

Where I worked, we gave our direct patient care staff free meals, set up a grocery store on campus with the basics so they could avoid going to more public grocery stores, and had "essential worker" bracelets made so that they could show law enforcement in case they were stopped on the street. We took care of our team; however, we all left work each day fearing we may be bringing COVID-19 home to our loved ones.

The financial success or failure of a treatment center falls upon the CEO. He or she must make difficult decisions for the good of the enterprise, often rendering them the least popular person in the building. Over time, however, their decisions usually prove to be right or at least necessary.

CEOs can assist families facing financial ruin. For example, several family members might require treatment, or there may be one who needs to return for treatment multiple times. A CEO can approve scholarships and discounts, but they must balance acts of generosity and compassion with sound fiscal decisions.

Sadly, there are some CEOs who operate from their ego rather than a sense of humility. They become enamored with their own power and utilize it for self-aggrandizement rather than for the good of their team and patients. This leads to rapid staff turnover, burnout, and dissatisfaction among teams, creating an unsafe environment for both employees and patients.

Other CEOs balance multiple priorities with grace and humility. They realize being responsible for the lives of the patients and their team is daunting and humbling. The best CEOs generate and maintain a positive culture within the treatment center. This creates a healthy, safe environment in which patients can heal and team members can grow.

Work It!

Devise questions to learn about founders and CEOs. These questions should be asked of your admissions or outreach person before you sign on the dotted line.

This can be done over the phone or via email. A trusted person can also do this for you, if it's too overwhelming. The answers to these questions should indicate a certain openness and trust in the culture of the program. Even if you don't quite understand the answers or find them meaningful in the context of your personal knowledge of the treatment field, you can open a dialogue and find a sense of connection and credibility through the questions and answers. Look for things like stability, tenure, and accountability.

Consider whether the person is forthcoming with information. Is there a legacy and history to be proud of? What is the tone when discussing leadership? Has leadership been in place for a while? How long has the person on the other end of the phone been working at the center? Some sample questions include the following:

1. How long has your facility been in business?
2. Who was, or is, the founder?
    - What can you tell me about them?
    - Are they involved on a day-to-day basis?
3. Who presently owns your center?
4. Who is your CEO/executive director?
    - Are they accessible to patients and families?
    - How long have they been in their role? What was their role prior?
5. What happens to the client if they are administratively discharged? What is the policy of the CEO for administrative discharges?

6. Do you have scholarships and discounts available, and does the CEO approve them?

Play 2: Learn About Your New Frontline Family

Role: The Primary Therapist

In established, professional treatment programs (both residential and outpatient), the primary therapist can change a patient's life, perhaps even save it. Ideally, they are a master's level clinician with an independent license. Licensure for a therapist/counselor requires three thousand-plus hours of supervised work by a credentialed professional. Many graduates of master's programs don't pursue licensure because it is difficult, time consuming, and expensive. The credentialing boards in various states don't make it easy, which only increases the credibility of our profession. (Not too long ago, someone could hang up a shingle, with no formal education or training, and call it therapy). Associate-level therapists are frequently found as primary therapists in both outpatient and residential programs. They can be quite effective when paired with a strong, independently licensed clinical supervisor.

People drawn to the role of primary therapist in a residential setting are often themselves in recovery from a substance use disorder or have a personal connection to the work because of a family member. Often more than 75 percent of the therapists on staff at a treatment center have a personal connection to the disease of a substance use disorder. In addition to their advanced degree, a primary therapist can obtain additional certifications and qualifications, for example in trauma or eating disorders, making them more effective at their job, especially when treating co-occurring disorders. (See chapter 4).

The primary therapist, ideally, spends at least eight hours per week with each resident in group and individual settings. It is often said a primary therapist goes where angels fear to tread, earning them the affectionate nicknames of "mind ninja," "Yoda," or "angel."

Having worked with some of the best primary therapists in the world, ages twenty-eight to seventy-eight, I can say that there is no expiration date on wisdom or shelf life for a gifted therapist. A good primary therapist can sit in someone else's pain and love them until they can love themselves. A patient once told their therapist that they had no hope for sobriety or a future because they had no higher power or belief in God. The therapist replied, "I'll pray to my God for you until you get one of your own." This forged an immediate, unbreakable connection between patient and therapist.

Ethically challenged therapists are also rampant. These therapists exploit their power over vulnerable patients in a variety of ways, from creating a personal relationship to borrowing money from them to engaging in a sexual relationship with them. One therapist even married a patient who she met while working in treatment. Therapists can lose their way and make poor decisions when struggling with burnout and compassion fatigue. Poor decisions not only harm patients but they can also derail a therapist's professional and personal life. Some are sued for malpractice or lose their license. You can research if there are any complaints against a therapist's license by going to the Board of Behavioral Health website in the state where they practice. If there is something on the website, I recommend that you ask someone in leadership at the program what the status is and then make the decision to discuss with your therapist or not.

Role: Medical Provider

When someone enters residential treatment, they are given three assessments: a history and physical, a psychiatric evaluation, and, as defined in Chapter 10, Treatment Components & Daily Schedule: The Plays for Working the Program, a biopsychosocial assessment. The history and physical and the psychiatric assessment are conducted by a medical provider (MP) with results serving as the clinical/medical roadmap for the patient's care. The medical provider makes the diagnosis and prescribes medication, if needed. If detoxification from drugs or alcohol is required, the MP oversees the detox process. During residential treatment, the MP meets with the patient weekly and makes referrals to the appropriate support providers upon their discharge.

Other responsibilities include designing a medication-assisted treatment plan, which may include methadone, buprenorphine, or naltrexone. Detoxification is a challenging process, so the MP is there to support patients through, while adjusting dosages of medications as needed and coordinating with other members of the team.

The MP has the highest level of training and licensure in the facility and is often looked at as the team captain. Meaning: they get the last word on decisions such as diagnosis, length of stay and leaving against medical advice. They meet regularly (at least weekly) with the treatment team (therapists, nurses, and so on) and make themselves available for consultations.

Medical doctors (MDs) and doctors of osteopathic medicine (DOs) receive more rigorous training than any other type of medical provider a treatment center might employ. MDs and DOs may select specialties, like psychiatry and addiction medicine, requiring a four-year residency program after medical school with the option of an additional one-to-two-year fellowship.

Due to the rising costs of MDs and DOs over the past several years, treatment programs have moved away from hiring MDs and DOs in favor of mid-level practitioners with prescribing authority and the ability to practice independently in most states. Mid-level practitioners include advanced practice registered nurses, physician associates/physician assistants, and doctors of nursing practice. These practitioners can deliver care of impeccable quality. Let's learn more about them.

Advanced practice registered nurse (APRN) is a term for nursing professionals who have earned a master's or doctoral degree in their quest to take on more advanced roles in the field of nursing. Although APRNs are not medical doctors and should not be referred to as "doctor," they can assess patients, render a diagnosis, and treat a wide range of medical conditions. They can order computerized axial tomography scans (better known as CAT scans), MRIs, X-rays, and blood work. APRNs can also prescribe medications and order medical equipment and home healthcare.

Physician associates/physician assistants are healthcare professionals educated at the master's degree level. Using a patient-centered, team-based approach to health and wellness, physician associates/physician assistants conduct physical exams, prescribe medications, develop treatment plans, provide education on preventive care, and may even assist in surgery. Their specific duties depend on their level of expertise and the clinical setting and state they work in.

A doctor of nursing practice is an individual with a doctorate degree in nursing, meaning he or she has obtained the highest level of education possible in the field of nursing.

Many of these doctors move on to leadership roles in the healthcare field. Some of them become psychiatric nurse practitioners and work as directors of drug treatment centers, psychiatric facilities, and rehabilitation centers. Doctors of nursing practice may work with local health agencies, schools, law enforcement, and the community to combat drug abuse and addiction.

Additionally, the MP determines when someone is cleared to leave treatment. While the MP works collaboratively with the team, he or she has the final say in all major decisions. After all, the MP has the highest level of licensure and the highest risk of personal liability.

After completing the assessments discussed above and in previous chapters, the medical provider looks at each patient—body, mind, and spirit—and provides counsel and solutions regarding major areas of their lives. For example, an MP will educate a patient on the role trauma plays in their chronic pain and how their brain consistently sends them the message "I hurt." The MP may uncover hormonal imbalances or other physiological conditions contributing to the patient's current psychological state. MPs, in collaboration with the other treatment team members, help patients build psychological resilience, allowing them to believe solutions can be found outside of a pain pill. These solutions may also take the form of exercise, massage, and insight-oriented work. In residential treatment, patients will see their medical provider weekly, and in outpatient, infrequently or not at all depending on the program, as the expectation is that they will follow up with their primary care provider.

Unfortunately, in the treatment community, there are medical providers that do not listen to their patients and push meds to address problematic behavior. Sadly, many people leave treatment with more prescription medications than they came in with. Being heavily medicated while in treatment makes it impossible to do the deep emotional work required for sustained recovery. The expression "snow them" means that an MP uses meds to take the edge off a problematic patient. Both residential and outpatient programs will have a medical provider on call in case of emergency. Most states require that the on-call medical provider be within an hour's driving distance of the facility, so that they can come as needed.

Work It!

Questions to ask your medical team

Primary Therapist

1. Do your therapists have master's level training? Are they independently licensed?

2. What percentage of your therapists are in recovery from a substance use disorder or mental illness?
3. What specialized training do they have?
4. What trauma training have they received? Do they utilize trauma-informed care?
5. Will family members get to speak to or meet with the primary therapist?
6. What is the average time that a therapist works at your program?
7. Are there programs in place to address burnout and compassion fatigue among staff?
8. Do any of your therapists have complaints filed against them for unprofessional conduct?

Medical Director

1. What are the credentials held by your medical director?
2. Do you have a psychiatrist and/or addictionologist on staff?
3. Are your MPs employed full time, and is there a medical staff member on site during normal business hours?
4. What is your on-call policy? Can the doctors be reached after hours, and will they come in, if necessary?
5. How many times per week do the MPs see each patient? What is the duration of the visit?

6. Do your MPs attend weekly meetings with the therapists?
7. How many mid-level practitioners are on staff, and are they supervised by an MD or DO?
8. Does your MP provide follow-up care? If so, what does it entail?

Role: Outreach Specialist

Many treatment centers hire outreach specialists (a.k.a. outreach reps, or ORR) to expand their reach, as the name implies. Some outreach specialists seek out people struggling within the local community, while others work in various locations throughout the state and country. Yes, patients come from near and far. The consensus among team members is that approximately half of the residents at any given treatment center reside within state while the other half come from out of state.

Unfortunately, outreach specialists have gotten a bad rap. The introduction of new legislation, along with the efforts of organizations like the National Association of Addiction Treatment Providers and Shatterproof, has changed the role of the ORR to one of community support and involvement. The ORRs I have worked with are caring and compassionate professionals that give their hearts and souls to helping people access treatment.

The outreach specialist guides and navigates patients to the program best suited for them clinically and financially. Several companies have created outreach and treatment placement specialist teams, which has improved the credibility of the role and restored trust to the position. The typical outreach specialist is in recovery, is a clinician, and has limitless perseverance and heart.

An outreach specialist can be the patient or family's first contact upon seeking treatment, often staying with the patient through all levels of care. They establish relationships within their communities and treatment programs, ensuring communication is ongoing and continued care is in place. Having someone to walk through the entire process with—having a *continuum of care*—is vital to the patient's long-term success. These may even be the people that you ask all of your questions! Their background and knowledge base are well-rounded enough to enable them to answer any question you might have.

On the human side of things, ORRs can be found on planes escorting their patients to treatment, staying near the center to ensure all is going well, or supporting a family in the middle of the night during a crisis. Wherever the ORR is included as part of the team, communication is improved, and the patient's experience is enhanced.

Community members place a great deal of trust in the ORR, whose reputation and good name is on the line when a placement is made. A sub-specialty within the ORR realm are Educational consultants. An Educational consultant, often provide support to families with adolescents who may need treatment in addition to support with secondary education choices. Like ORR, they are knowledgeable and supportive professionals with the best interest of the family as their top priority.

Role: Behavioral Health Tech

The tech is on the front lines—the first person you see when you walk in the door and the last person you see when you are discharged from care. Techs are usually in recovery and have been patients themselves. Since the tech works where the patient lives, they are the eyes and ears of the treatment team and will share concerns immediately, such as if a patient is missing group meetings and/or isolating in their room. Working 24/7, the tech is the one who provides a listening ear at 3 a.m. when a patient can't sleep or who takes them on a walk after a tough call with the family.

Acting also as a rule enforcer, the tech ensures patients don't sneak their phones back into their rooms or enter romantic relationships with their peers. Rehab romances are common but dangerous. Often, when a coping mechanism like drugs, alcohol, or food is taken away, it will be replaced with something else that provides a rush of feel-good dopamine to the brain. Rehab romances are also known as "911" relationships because most result in a call to 911 within six to twelve months.

The role of the tech can be enormously stressful but rewarding as they have the trust of both patients and staff. Perhaps all students, during college or immediately after, might benefit from spending six months working as a tech in a residential setting. Why? It is a role that fosters the development of empathy, boundaries, and street smarts. Plus, it helps dismantle the stigma of addiction and mental illness. My own daughter worked the night shift (6 p.m. to 6 a.m.) in a residential treatment program for six months between her senior year of college and starting her full-time job. The experience profoundly impacted and broadened her worldview and gave her a new perspective on addiction and mental health issues.

The techs, responsible for patient tracking and safety, are either part of the clinical or the nursing organization. Hero techs are fearless. They have been known to run into the street to retrieve a fleeing patient, boldly putting their patients' lives before their own. Irresponsible techs (often under poor supervision) may take advantage of the time between midnight and 6 a.m. (a.k.a. the "deep night") to sleep on the job, help themselves to medication, or "hook up" with another staff member, or worse yet, a patient. These are the reasons techs receive training in boundaries and supervision, as do all members of the treatment team.

Techs are often in school studying to become counselors, nurses, and even medical doctors. Since COVID-19, the greatest challenge in running a treatment center has been staffing key positions. The tech position is the most challenging to fill. Jobs at Amazon, or in other non-behavioral health environments, are readily available for more money and better benefits. Fortunately, many treatment programs provide higher hourly rates and other retention tools to keep staff from looking for employment elsewhere. Programs that cannot retain quality staff are faced with using agency workers untrained for the specific environment of addiction recovery.

Role: Nurse

Nurses in residential treatment centers play a vital role during the admission process. The nurse does the initial physical assessment, takes the patient's vitals, reviews medications, and performs skin checks to look for rashes, cuts, and bruises. The nurse decides if the patient has any emergent medical issues that might warrant a trip to the hospital. Like techs, nurses work where the patients live and see them daily for medication and medical care. Most insurance companies require residential facilities to have twenty-four-hour nursing care, a key component of quality care.

There are various levels of nursing credentials, from licensed practical nurse, or LPN, with a two-year degree, to a registered nurse, or RN, with a three-year degree, to a Bachelor of Science in Nursing, or BSN, with a four-year degree. Many nurse leaders also have a Master of Nursing Administration. Again, the post COVID-19 world is experiencing unprecedented staff shortages, and nursing is no exception. Many centers are unable to cover their shifts without nurses working several shifts in a row. Some rely on agency nurses to cover specific shifts and/or traveling nurses who might spend a few months at that location before moving on.

Nurses play a vital role in helping patients tune into their physical health and well-being. Nurses also support patients in addressing issues that can derail their recovery, such as pain and sleep deprivation. Like techs, nurses are with patients around the clock and develop strong relationships with them.

Work It!

Here are some questions to ask your ORR, tech, and nurse:

ORR

1. What is the background and training of the ORR?
2. How are they compensated?
3. Do you purchase plane tickets for patients?
4. What is your policy on the length of sobriety for hiring employees?

Behavioral Health Tech

1. What training and/or education does your front-line staff have?
2. Who supervises the techs?
3. Are your techs in recovery, and how long of a sobriety period do they need before being hired?
4. What is the rate of turnover for your direct patient care staff?

Nurse

1. Do you have twenty-four-hour nursing staff?
2. What are the credentials of your nurses?
3. Do you use agency or traveling nurses?

Play 3. Meet the Special Teams

Although not clinical or direct patient care team members, there are some key individuals who contribute to the success of the treatment experience.

Role: Alumni Coordinator

The alumni coordinator can be a beacon of hope to a patient while in treatment and a lifeline after they leave. Alumni coordinators are usually in recovery and have been patients themselves.

The alumni coordinator meets with patients during treatment and reinforces the importance of a continued connection after discharge. If a patient has a positive experience while in treatment, the treatment center becomes their "safe place." Having someone reach out to them once they are out is a vital component of quality care.

The alumni coordinator ensures that the patient is called within twenty-four to forty-eight hours after discharge and provides regular follow-ups via phone calls, visits, email, and social media. They also host informative and fun events, as well as an annual retreat. Retreats bring alumni together regardless of whether they were discharged from treatment recently or thirty years ago.

Hero alumni coordinators (and most are) intervene when someone is in crisis, sending police in when necessary. They are there when someone begins to struggle, so a slipup does not become a relapse, and suicidal ideation doesn't become an attempt. Their unique position makes them the bearers of both good and tragic news. By keeping in touch with patients long term, alumni coordinators hear about victories and triumphs. They are also the first to know when an alumnus doesn't make it. In those instances, they provide support to the bereaved family members and heartbroken team members who care deeply about the patient.

Alumni coordinators are not clinicians. They rely on their peer-support training and life experiences to help keep alumni connected to a meaningful life in recovery.

Work It!

To learn more about the long-term benefits of the rehab center of your choice, ask the following questions. It has been found that the more substantial an alumni program, the more engaged and less likely to relapse a patient is. We will cover alumni programs more fully in the last chapter of this book.

1. Do you have an alumni program?
2. Are you members of TPAS? (Treatment Professionals in Alumni Services)
3. What does your alumni program entail?
4. Do you have alumni coordinators?
5. What is their background?
6. How soon and how often do they call patients after discharge?
7. Do you have an annual event?

Role: The Chef

Food is love. Chefs who are employed in residential treatment centers could be making a lot more money working in restaurants. Instead, they gravitate toward a setting where their talents, passion, and understanding of the role of food in healing can be put to good use. Chefs working in residential centers have been known to bake treats for staff during difficult times. They also strive to accommodate the various nutritional and cultural needs of the patients and staff.

Through my years in the field, I have worked with many great chefs, but one really stands out: Chef Bill. He and I worked together to create and implement "Family Dinner" where patients ate with their process group family-style rather than the standard buffet. Chef Bill stood side by side with administrative staff members, watching and listening with pride, as several patients revealed that they had never eaten as a family before. He beamed when his specially prepared meals were appreciated and celebrated. He has since passed on, but no one will forget his compassion and generosity of spirit.

Role: The Housekeeper

Keeping a treatment center clean, before, during, and after COVID-19 is a challenge. These dedicated team members change beds in a snap, mop up endless spills, and become the crowd favorite of patients and staff alike. Sometimes, it is their smile, grace, or a compassionate word or prayer that gets everyone through an awful day.

I have worked in many facilities over the years and known dozens of outstanding housekeepers. My favorite one prayed nightly for my husband when he had a heart attack and ran to the car to greet him when he got out of the hospital. When I resigned my position as CEO, I wanted to be the one to tell her. She cried, and we sat quietly holding hands. We both appreciated how hard the other worked and the friendship we had developed.

Role: The Transporter

Since many folks travel for treatment, programs either have transportation departments or transport designees. Transport personnel are the angels found waiting to greet their new arrivals at the airport's baggage claim. They are, in fact, the first staff members patients lay eyes on as they embark on their recovery journey. The gentle compassion displayed by the transport team can put a patient right at ease, making all the difference in the world. Often retired, transport personnel enjoy bringing new patients into treatment and view their job as their renewed purpose in life.

Role: The Horse

Equine therapy incorporates horses as part of the therapeutic process. Along with more traditional approaches, interacting with horses can help people express and regulate their emotions, build self-confidence, and develop a sense of responsibility.

Equine therapy is widely used in treatment programs across the country. Over the past decade, it has evolved as a treatment modality requiring professional certifications and licensure. The larger, more elaborate programs have on-site stables and herds, while smaller programs transport their patients to local stables.

Patients may groom, feed, or lead a horse while being supervised by a mental health counselor trained in equine therapy.

As large prey animals, horses survive by two means: their intuition and their herd. Their own life experiences allow them to provide information and insight not available through traditional talk therapy. The effectiveness of equine therapy may be a result of interacting with such a magnificent animal or a result of the horse's own soul and life stories. Horses have the uncanny ability to mirror a patient's emotions, revealing their fears, trauma, and stories of distrust in relationships.

Circle of Support

When the transport van from the treatment center pulled up to the stable where I practiced equine therapy, a patient would frequently look at a horse, usually the biggest one, and declare, "That horse hates me." It wasn't always easy to get patients to understand that the horse had no feeling about them and was only reflecting their emotions back to them—like looking in the mirror. The ability to get that message across to a patient was a huge accomplishment, one capable of breaking through long-held beliefs and decades of self-loathing behaviors.

One horse, named Klyk, was particularly talented as a therapist. His story included being an Arabian show horse who, while gifted and successful, could not consistently perform at the levels expected of him. This inability to meet the expectations of his trainers and former owners put him in life-threatening situations, leading him to act out in a variety of ways. They retired him at a young age.

Luckily, Klyk was selected to work as an equine therapy horse. His easygoing, gentle manner was a soothing balm to those patients most broken while his size and confidence challenged those who entered the arena with arrogance and aggression. Klyk and his story resonated with many addicts in treatment, and he saved countless lives through his work.

Klyk also taught one young girl, my daughter, who called him her own for twenty years, about unconditional love. He was a beloved member of the treatment team and our family until his giant heart stopped beating at the age of thirty.

For Fans and Family

Compassion fatigue is the emotional physical distress caused by treating and helping patients that are deeply in need, a.k.a. "The Cost of Caring." Professionals experiencing compassion fatigue may find it difficult to continue doing their jobs. They become disillusioned with their work and jaded, and it's fair to say that are not at the top of their game, personally or professionally.

Often people with compassion fatigue suffer from burnout or emotional exhaustion and have a low sense of personal accomplishment. Another component of compassion fatigue is secondary traumatic stress, which occurs when exposed to another person's trauma. Many healthcare organizations, especially since COVID-19, have worked hard to implement programs to support their teams to prevent burnout and compassion fatigue by giving them encouragement and tools to practice self-care. Finding out if the program you are researching offers support for therapists is a worthwhile question when making your selection.

TEAM MEETING

Interview with Nicholas Kardaras, PhD, LCSW-R, Psychologist, Speaker, Digital Addiction Expert, Author, Founder/CEO of Omega Recovery, Austin and Maui Recovery, Hawaii

Jaime Vinck: Nick, thank you so much for joining me in a discussion about the impact teams have on the rehabilitation process. The whole idea behind this section of *The Rehab Playbook* is honoring the people doing the quiet work and highlighting the power of the team. Obviously, none of us does this alone. Why do you believe the team is so important?

NK: I've been a clinician, and I've run programs. I've also been through treatment. I've been through treatment a lot. Before I got my shit together, it used to be a running joke that I was a frequent flier. I went to multiple detoxes and rehabs. By multiple, I mean over double digits before it stuck.

When I was a client, I was impacted by teams. There were so many mustard seeds planted by so many. In one program, it was a custodian who said, "Come on, kid, you know, give yourself a break and forgive yourself." We would talk informally, and his words of support and positivity really meant a lot to me during that treatment stay. Of course, the therapist takes the lead. I had a therapist who was not in recovery herself but who could connect and be compassionate. I'd like to think [that] she was the reason [that] the shift happened, but everybody on down was part of the process, part of the equation.

When I had the opportunity to run the team, I included everyone in clinical meetings who had touches [interactions] with clients. We would have everybody, from the cleaning staff to the outside contractors. They had limited work with the patients but had some of the most important touch. Support staff, certainly, were the eyes and ears of the program. The clinicians saw the most inauthentic presentation during the therapy session, but the support staff saw the clients with the curtain pulled back. They saw them in their natural habitat when they weren't trying to perform for the therapist.

When I ran The Dunes, we had a chef there who was more of a therapist than the therapists. Most of the clients mentioned him in their exit surveys, how they could talk to him and how understanding he was. Our dining area was open to the kitchen, so the clients always wandered over to him while he was chopping onions or preparing the meal.

He was a younger guy from an Italian family, a great listener. He gave people support, and everybody felt their relationship with him was important. When we would thank him for the phenomenal things he was doing for the clients in addition to the food, he would say, "I don't know anything about therapy. I'm just being a human here."

There were other moments of pure magic when we least expected it. I remember one specific snapshot. We had a twenty-seven or twenty-eight-year-old young woman, a serious crystal meth addict, let's call her Julie, who was the daughter of one of the most prominent cardiologists in New York. Good family and great upbringing, but she had fallen into bad habits. Julie was running with wolves and had been living a hard life for five or six years. She was hard core with all the wear and tear on her body of a crystal meth addict. When Julie came into our program, hardened and angry, few people held out hope for her recovery.

We did a lot of different, experiential stuff as Dr. [Howard] Shaffer from Harvard was helping us develop some of our programming. He embraced what was called the "syndrome model," where you throw a lot of different therapies to people because you don't know which is going to be the magical piece.

I've seen hedge fund intellectuals reduced to tears by art therapy [that] they never wanted to do. Then I've seen artists who needed to do something more intellectual. You never know what's going to work.

Back to Julie. One day, she went on an evening walk with one of our support staff. They wanted to go off the property near a beach to see the sun set. She came back crying and couldn't stop for about an hour. When we asked what was wrong, she said nothing was wrong; she had just never seen anything so beautiful in her life. She was so moved by the beauty of the sunset and really hadn't been in her senses, or in her clarity, in years.

She cried tears of joy for herself and tears of sadness for those who were missing out and still struggling. After that experience, she went from being a rough and tumble "I don't want to do this" client to "I'm all in." The person who had accompanied her was a support staff who happened to be the ideal, gentle sherpa for the walk Julie went on. Nobody had expected any change, let alone something of this magnitude.

So Julie wanted to go on the walk, and this female tech, who happened to be on the schedule, was at the right place with just the right temperament to help her experience the sunset that created the seismic shift she needed. I'm sure her therapist tilled the soil and other things happened to make her receptive to the experience but that walk with that support staff member was her turning point. She had been a hardened client who had prostituted herself and done all these horrible things, and she shifted. It's beautiful. Nine or ten years later, from what I understand, she is still doing well.

CHAPTER 7

WEIGHING THE OPTIONS

The Plays for Making Key Considerations for Your Care

"Choices are the hinges of destiny."

—EDWIN MARKHAM

Regardless of the type of program you choose or is chosen for you, having a voice in your treatment experience and input into your goals will be important to your lasting recovery. You've met the key players in the process, voiced your concerns, and interviewed them to learn as much as you can about what to expect. We've assessed your level of care and the options available to meet your needs. However, there are more nuanced considerations, ones that are concerned with your lived experiences, preferences, and personal characteristics. This chapter continues the dialogue as you search for the right treatment program, so you can keep the things that are personally important to you top of mind. Things like culture, age, vocation, gender, location, and accreditation are all key considerations that add depth to your journey. As you'll see, when it comes to your options, there's lots of things to weigh.

Play 1. Weigh Quality and Safety

The most important things to consider when weighing your options are quality and safety. A quality program will be licensed by the state in which they are located and are accredited either by the Joint Commission or the Commission on Accreditation of Rehabilitation Facilities, or CARF, accreditation. To earn these accreditations means that the treatment centers have met strict requirements and gone through and passed a comprehensive review process of all major areas of their treatment program. The survey will include auditing the kitchen (such as the even temperature of the refrigerator) and fire drill protocols to name a few, as well as doing a deep dive on all clinical services.

Both the individual states and the accrediting body field patient complaints that are fully investigated. Any citations resulting from the complaints are a matter of public record. You can find them on your state's behavioral health licensing website. The best way to find out if there are any citations is to ask in your preadmission process. Please keep in mind that the regulatory bodies are the patient's advocates and allies. They hold us, as operators, accountable and keep the standards high. At the end of every Joint Commission or state audit that I have been part of, no matter the tone and outcome, I express gratitude for their role in helping us improve our patient care. That is why we are all here.

Considering safety regarding your specific needs based on your history and clinical needs is also an important part of this play. Having input into your own treatment plan and agency in your own life is critical to your success. Treatment, while often inconvenient and the road getting there is not pleasant, can and will be the greatest gift of your life if you allow it. The best way to make that happen is to have a voice in the decision. In your search for treatment, you may come across programs that are not licensed or accredited. These programs may appear lovely, be in great locations, and have a number of attractive amenities. Please keep in mind that not only are these programs unregulated, but they will also not be eligible for insurance reimbursement. Getting on an insurance panel requires licensure and many require accreditation.

Play 2. Weigh Cultural Competence

Another critical component in weighing options is the program's cultural competence. According to Ashlee Wisdom, MPH [master of public health], CEO, and founder of Health in Her HUE, cultural competence in therapy is:

- "Care that is given to a patient that takes into account their lived experiences and their social and cultural contexts."
- "Seeing all aspects of a patient and taking into account the things that they value."

In other words, cultural competence in therapy involves a mental health professional understanding the beliefs, backgrounds, and values of their clients—this includes their culture, race, ethnicity, religion, gender socioeconomic status, and sexuality.

Even if you don't have a shared experience with your therapist, feeling that they are doing their best to understand your world is essential in building trust, which means they are displaying "cultural humility." Cultural humility is rooted in respect, as well as the acknowledgment and awareness of privilege.

In a 2021 article called "Cultural Considerations in Addiction Treatment," authors Connie Jones and Susan Branco shared that "Ignoring the diverse needs of clients is neglectful and does not support effective treatment outcomes. Further, providers who strive to incorporate cultural humility in their work allow opportunities for treatment relationships to strengthen and withstand any ruptures that may arise along the course of treatment. In turn, clients receive culturally sensitive care and quality overall treatment services."

Play 3. Weigh Specialized Programs

Specialized programs in addiction and recovery are tailored treatment approaches that address the unique and shared needs of certain populations. They can also target particular aspects of addiction and recovery and even drugs of choice. Specialized programs include a range of populations based on age, career, type of trauma, culture, race, gender, and sexual preference. It has been found that identifying with others in treatment can increase the likelihood of successful, lasting recovery for individuals with diverse needs and backgrounds.

The following are examples of specialized programs and why these might be the answer for you:

Programs based on age

Young adult—programs for ages eighteen to twenty-five are focused on the challenges unique to this age group. In addition to the drugs of choice, they often focus on failure to launch, tech/screen addiction, and anxiety. There is typically a great deal of family involvement and support.

Mature adult—programs for ages 55 and above are often referred to as older adults or seniors programs. In addition to drugs of choice, they often focus on grief, depression, chronic pain, and finding meaning and purpose. The family involvement here often varies and can range from none (all loved ones are gone) to "helicopter kids" terrified of losing their parent to angry adult kids that don't want to see their inheritance being spent on their parents' treatment.

Programs based on gender

Women's programs are specialized environments that provide a safe setting where women can focus on their recovery without the distractions or pressures that might come from a coed treatment setting. In addition to their drugs of choice, they often focus on sexual abuse, trauma, and relationship issues. These issues are approached with sensitivity and with a level of openness and vulnerability that is crucial for healing. Family involvement varies depending on the nature of the current relationship and history.

Men's programs are specialized environments that provide a supportive and understanding setting where men can also focus on their recovery without the distractions or pressures that might come from a coed treatment setting. In addition to their drugs of choice, they often focus on trauma, anger management, sexuality, and healthy masculinity. There is also an opportunity for increased fellowship and support in all-male setting. Family work varies based on the status of their relationships and history.

Many gender-specific treatment programs also recognize the unique challenges that LGBTQ+ individuals face, which often makes their recovery journey feel even lonelier. LGBTQ+ specialized programs (either stand alone or within a larger program) offer a safe space for LGBTQ+ men and women to feel heard, supported, and validated during their treatment and recovery journey.

"Specialized programs include a range of populations based on age, career, type of trauma, culture, race, gender, and sexual preference. It has been found that identifying with others in treatment can increase the likelihood of successful, lasting recovery for individuals with diverse needs and backgrounds."

The National Institute on Drug Abuse offers suggestions when searching for LGBTQ+ culturally competent care. Remember, you should not feel like you need to educate providers about the basic concepts of LGBTQ+ identities. To prevent that, consider asking the following questions:

- My identity is ______________________________.
  What experience do you have working with people with that identity?
- What experience do you have with the LGBTQ+ community?

- Do you have any specific training or certifications that relate to working with LGBTQ+ clients?

Additionally, National Institute on Drug Abuse recommends that in order to avoid selecting a practitioner that uses the discredited and harmful practice of conversion or reparative therapy—aimed at changing a person's sexual orientation or gender identity—you may also want to ask, "Do you provide conversion therapy or reparative therapy?" and follow up by asking how they feel about that specific practice to make sure you are not selecting a provider that advocates for this type of treatment.

Many coed programs do a fine job in offering gender-separate housing and process groups, creating the safety needed to address issues effectively. Some go so far as to have a "no fraternizing" policy, where men and women are not allowed to sit together at meals or during group activities. Programs make this decision because of the reality of "rehab romances." It's all too common for patients to fall in love with someone in treatment. This occurs because once the drug of choice is taken away, another "feel good" action replaces it. The intensity of the experiences creates an immediate rush, and the romance (and often a sexual relationship) begins. It's a distraction from the hard work. I'm usually told, "Nobody 'gets' you like someone who went to treatment with you." While I have heard of one or two of these relationships working out, most often they do not. When rehab is over, the intensity fades, and all that is left are two people, relative strangers, both new to sobriety, trying to navigate recovery. Relapse is likely inevitable in a rehab romance story.

At the risk of over simplifying, if you know that you are more comfortable sharing personal stories and being emotionally vulnerable around people of the same gender, a gender-separate program, in full or in part, is for you. If you know that you tend to seek romantic/sexual attention when feeling vulnerable, regardless of your sexuality, advise your therapist when you check in. Your therapist may put you on a "grubby contact" (baggy clothes, minimal grooming) so that you are less likely to sexualize while in treatment.

Programs based on careers

There are also programs dedicated to various professions, like physicians, nurses, first responders, flight attendants, safety-sensitive positions, veterans, and so on, or tracks within a larger program. The advantage of these specialized tracks is the ability to process information with those who have had similar experiences, backgrounds, and challenges. A disadvantage is that limiting your exposure to those who have had the lived experience that you have had may not necessarily broaden your perspective or worldview.

Many employers have employee assistance programs that influence the decision of when it's time for someone to go to treatment and direct where the employee will go. The employee assistance program often selects three programs that they know are a good fit with their employees, are known to the employee assistance program, and provide quality care. The ultimate decision is with the potential patient, and the tips in this section will help in making the final selection.

Programs based on location preferences

Another key decision is to stay in your own geographic area or go to a destination "fly away" program. This decision is often dictated by what is covered by insurance, and there are arguments for both. Some patients prefer to go to treatment in their hometown so that their family can be involved and that they can see them frequently. There is also an advantage to continuing your care and support groups in your own community, because longer-term relationships and connections can be made on your home turf. Something to be aware of in the local community model is anonymity. It is possible that in seeking treatment in your community, you may find yourself face-to-face with your high school sweetheart's brother, someone that you treated or arrested (if a healthcare professional or first responder), or someone from your church. I have seen all of these occur with varying treatment implications, and I recommend that you discuss what happens in these situations prior to admissions. For example, if you are directly or indirectly acquainted with someone in your group, will accommodations be made?

Many treatment professionals prefer that the patient is away from their home turf, creating distance from the people, places, and things that have triggered use. This thought process is why there are many treatment centers in temperate climates such as Arizona, Florida, and California.

Programs Based on Support Groups

In a later chapter, we will discuss the various support groups that are available. Evidence supports 12-step programs, and there are fine programs that are based solely on them. You will also find programs that claim to be "non-12-step" and do offer some of the other support groups, including the SMART Recovery program, which is also supported by science. The programs where I have worked, and ones I have built, offer both. I have seen anti-12-step patients return to treatment and fall in love with the 12-step community the second time around. I have seen 12-step fans return to treatment and decide that they needed to add the Refuge Recovery and SMART Recovery programs to their plan. The truth is that we don't know when someone is going to get their miracle, so making several support options available has been my preferred approach.

Circle of Support

With all of the options there are to consider for treatment, it is truly amazing how the universe often gives us exactly what we need through our peers in group therapy.

I once worked with a middle-aged man who was self-medicating with alcohol and destroying his family and career. No one could understand why he was drinking himself to death. In group, he shared that as a teen, he and his girlfriend became pregnant. They wanted to get married, but their families forced them to give the baby up for adoption. Had they refused, they would have been denied financial support and an education. Heartbroken, they agreed to give up their baby and soon went separate ways. This was the source of the man's pain, the wound he could not drink away. Frozen in his heart, mind, and soul was the image of his seventeen-year-old self, staring through the hospital window at the baby boy he would never know. Could he ever be forgiven for giving his son up? Could he forgive himself?

Ironically, a young man in the group, barely twenty years old, was on the other end of an adoption issue. He had been a successful high school athlete and student but sustained a football injury that required oxycodone for the pain. The moment he swallowed his first pill, a deep emotional pain he had been hiding for years faded into the distance. He forgot his shame and self-loathing until the dose wore off. What was his wound? Guilt and abandonment. Although he adored his adoptive parents and was grateful for the wonderful life they gave him, he was consumed by the mystery of his biological parents. Why would they give him up? Would his birth father be proud of his many accomplishments?

The young man was obsessed with knowing if his biological dad cared enough to miss him, yet thinking if his dad really cared, he would have never let him go. The irony of these two stories was not lost on the group. Everyone wondered if we had both the biological father and son there together, yet unbeknownst to each other.

We did not. However, these two men worked together, sharing deep feelings of loss and abandonment. Over time, they learned to forgive and hastened each other's recovery.

Play 4. Assess your Relationship with Electronics

When weighing your options and making your decisions, be sure to fully understand the electronics policy of the program. It's also important that your family member understands and buys in.

When I first started working in treatment in 2005, someone having access to their computer or cell phone was unheard of. A few years later, the program where I worked opened a facility targeted at executives/professionals who "needed" and received unlimited access to their electronics.

I have had a ringside seat to the evolution of electronics use in treatment. I've seen it move from being strictly forbidden, to supervised phone use for the sole purpose of communicating with family and essential personal/professional business, to completely open use other than in group. This has been, and still is, a regularly debated topic among program operators, and there is still no consensus on overall best practices covering an entire treatment episode. The "digital detox" or "black out" when someone first gets to treatment (five to ten days) is widely accepted as best practice. Unplugging completely is meant to isolate you from the stressors of everyday life, as well as any potential damage that you may not want to deal with.

Looking at your relationship with electronics and social media and deciding if it's healthy or not can be an invaluable and unexpected bonus to seeking treatment. Phones can contain a lot of potentially triggering information, including phone numbers of dealers and voicemail messages from friends who are using. I have spent many sessions going through phones (and social media) with patients while in treatment, cleaning up the messages from the past in a supportive environment. In an attempt to encourage healthy electronic use, most programs encourage face time communication with children and will support any communication that furthers your recovery. You will also be able to pay bills and attend to other essential matters.

Work It!

If you have increased anxiety and fear about not having access to your phone, there are a few steps you can take to check out your use. The following is an illuminating thought experiment from Mayo Clinic Mental Health to answer the simple question—Do you use your smartphone too much? Test yourself and find out:

- **Step 1:** On a piece of paper, without looking it up, write down the estimated amount of time you spend per day on your phone.
- **Step 2:** Go to the "Screen Time" feature, typically located in the settings app on your phone. What is the daily average?

If there was a noticeable difference between your estimated screen time and your actual screen time, you're in good company. On average, Americans unlock their phone 160 times a day (every nine minutes!) and spend over five hours online daily. Perhaps most surprisingly, they underestimate their smartphone usage by 40 percent compared to their actual use.

If your results caused any concerns, please continue.

"To address the growing threat of smartphone addiction, researchers at the University of Toronto, Harvard University, and McGill University have launched a resource called Healthy Screens to help people better assess their smartphone use and take basic steps to improve their relationship to technology.

On the site (www.healthyscreens.com/scale), you can take a three-minute version of the Smartphone Addiction Scale to measure your own smartphone habits. If your results are concerning, you can discuss this further with your treatment team."

For Fans and Families

Many times, when a family agrees that someone needs treatment, there is a difference of opinion on who gets to make the call on which program to use. With compromise, cool heads, and often help from a professional, this situation can be navigated. The most important thing to remember is that there is an agreement to go to treatment and that is something to be celebrated. The fact that a particular person or people are paying doesn't give them the right to choose the program; they are not the ones who are going to do the work. Having each person make a list of the non-negotiables is a great way to start. Be clear on the areas that you are not prepared to compromise on. You deserve it, and it will help you not go into this process full of resentment. From there, we can seek to understand where there is a meeting of the minds and where we have conflict.

For example, one set of parents want their son out of the state, and the son wanted to stay at home to be near his girlfriend. Acknowledging the importance of the son's relationship, while reinforcing the need to be away from his stomping grounds, was a good place to start. Encouraging their son to share other factors that were important to him, such as climate, activities, and being around other people in his age group allowed him to exercise his choices. Letting their son use his voice to choose a program that has components that are important to him may make up for the parents' nonnegotiable of him leaving town.

In this case, I recommended that the son make the phone calls to intake and that the parents do not do it for him, allowing him to own the experience from the beginning. Being willing to compromise and granting the potential patient agency, even if we think that our loved one is in a diminished state, can go a long way to start the treatment episode off on the right foot.

Family and supporting each other—especially caregivers—throughout a loved one's recovery journey is the subject of the next chapter.

CHAPTER 8

FAMILY MATTERS

The Plays for Advocating for Your Own Healing—A Chapter for Caregivers

"Just for today, I will trust the ones who held me up, not the ones who let me down."

—AL-ANON

Staring across the auditorium of the treatment center, I saw a sea of faces staring back at me, offering an assortment of expressions. Confusion, frustration, skepticism, fear, angst, desperation, anger, sorrow, disgust, jadedness, and even numbness were like anchors on these people's souls. I recognized the weight of their feelings firsthand from my own personal experiences growing up with addiction, and I knew it professionally. All ages and walks of life were present, a confirmation that addiction doesn't care about demographics, creed, sex, or race.

Of all the emotions I decoded, I knew as I greeted this audience for the very first time that my priority was to tend to the greatest and most afflicting emotion of all—the gripping feeling they all shared in common—*hopelessness*.

These forty people were not here seeking treatment from their substance use disorder. These faces with the furrowed brows and the frowning mouths, the worn skin and the tired eyes, these weary people were the family members.

Every Monday, fifty-two weeks a year for five years, it was my great honor to welcome between twenty and forty family members who were spending a few days with their loved ones in the treatment center. They were embarking on their own journeys in what we called the "Family Program."

Each family member was dealing with their own post-traumatic stress from living their lives loving someone with a substance use disorder. It would be difficult to break through the anger and fear that barricaded them from allowing even the slightest bit of hope that their child, spouse, parent, sibling, or friend could find freedom from their substance use disorder. As a way in, I shared with them my own story of being an adult child of an alcoholic and my own struggles with depression. I related to their experiences, and I wanted them to know as such, so I told them that in high school I would come home from my after-school job and count the number of beer cans in the trash, which would tell me what version of Mom I would get when she woke up.

I wanted the family members to know that I too saw patterns of addiction, generations of people who needed help and never got it. I shared with them that my mom was doing great compared to her mom—because her mom used to get drunk and chase her around with a butcher knife. I'm living proof that cycles of intergenerational trauma, addiction, and abuse can be broken. While I'm not a perfect mom, my kids have never been afraid that I would be too drunk to take care of them or become violent with them. It's progress, not perfection. I challenged the family members to hope, to believe that they and their loved ones were in the right place at the right time and with tools, support, and faith, they'd come to understand so much during our time together.

Too many people with a substance use disorder seeking treatment of any level have suffered for years, silently and tragically. Many have hit their rock bottoms, and those rock bottoms are oftentimes hurting someone they love. Someone like you. Families who have stood by and watch their loved one spiral have suffered as silently and tragically as the person who is using. They need help too. Family matters. They too have experienced a trauma that required a reaction, typically, a prolonged and unhealthy fight, flight, or freeze response. Interactions become dysfunctional, chaos becomes the air they breathe, and boundaries are crossed and then erased.

In my experience, it isn't until a person is in treatment that the family sees that they too need guidance and support and finally have an opportunity to seek it. And even then, they might not know. Families are usually so immersed in the dramas and problems their loved ones are either causing or succumbing to that they don't see that they need healing too. They also need to learn to protect themselves from the ramifications of often toxic circumstances, coping strategies to manage stress, and how to release guilt in order to set boundaries and reclaim their own lives that have been commandeered by their loved one with a substance use disorder. And as discussed in an earlier chapter, many times during treatment, family members learn for the first time about traumas or adverse childhood events their loved one has been trying to avoid. This can be painful and difficult to process, another reason family members should be receiving tools and help. Because the impact on family members is so great, thankfully, it has become standard practice for individual-based treatment to include family education and multifamily groups.

Throughout the chapters of this book, I have dedicated sections specifically for family members, because let's face it, they are usually the ones orbiting their loved ones throughout the various cycles of their addiction—paying the emotional, physical, financial, and spiritual consequences. You might be the family member who bought this book for your loved one. And perhaps you are the only one who has cracked it open.

Regardless of what brought you here, this chapter is for you. Full disclosure, it won't teach you what you need to do specifically to heal your pain or to help your loved one. This chapter will not save your family or reinvent it. That's what treatment is for. But I do hope this chapter will introduce you and prepare you to learn some of the concepts and themes that will be raised once you receive the education you—the person on the frontlines—is entitled to. Your education and treatment will be much more worthwhile and lasting when you're primed and prepared for what's to come as you explore your role, recognize patterns, learn communication tools, admit mistakes, and gain a deeper understanding of not just the causes of your loved one's addiction, but of the toll it's taken on you. You might get your life back, along with your loved one. You might even experience...joy.

Play 1. Make Hope a Strategy

Hope has been a spiritual matter for eons; however, in the last few decades, scientists have been studying the clinical power of hope when it comes to overcoming adversity of any kind. It turns out hope *is* a strategy.

Supporting your loved one's treatment journey while nurturing your own education and therapy begins with a hope mindset. Again, I've seen this emotion as last on the minds of family members, but it is the required starting point. Hope can be hard to embrace because it makes us vulnerable to the possibility of future disappointment. *We just can't be defeated again*, we think. Still, as scary as it might be to let ourselves hope, it is a leap we must learn to take for the sake of ourselves and those we love.

Books, articles, and original research abound when it comes to learning even the smallest ways we can begin making hope our strategy for healing. I've drawn from many resources to tailor my own quick and general list of things to try on your own, adapt, or share with those who might need a little hope to keep them steady.

1. **Don't look back.** The present moment is all we have. There is no hope to be found in the pain of our past experiences, and if we stay in those negative places, we can never move forward. It's not easy to let the past go, especially if you've been burned and betrayed by your loved one or if you have almost lost them altogether. But being optimistic about where you are now and recognizing that you have survived what has already

transpired will help you see the hope that you are strong enough to be right here, right now.

2. **Forgive.** Related to letting go of the past is the act of forgiveness. As you say goodbye to all that has transpired, can you find a way to forgive, whether it be your loved one or yourself? Releasing the blame that you might be placing on yourself for the pain and suffering all parties have endured makes way for the hope of a new day. It breeds optimism, and optimism and hope go along like donuts and coffee. Forgiveness is not saying a transgression is okay or permissible. But it does say that you can accept what has happened without holding onto it or worse, letting it hold on to you and sinking your heart deeper and deeper away from the light of hope.
3. **Don't Set Yourself Up to Fail.** What are you hoping for? Maybe you have a goal you'd like to reach for yourself or your loved one. Achieving goals ignites hope. But the opposite is also true: nothing sets hope back like a failed attempt at a goal. Set goals small, make them realistic, and make them purposely reachable. Once you gain momentum of the achievement after achievement, you'll find that your hope muscle is developing and build confidence. With confidence comes more hope—and faith that the big goal, when you are ready to set it, will be achieved.
4. **Find hopeful people and stick to them like glue.** Energy is transferable. Who hasn't been in a room with a negative person and wanted to smudge themselves clean of

"It's progress, not perfection."

their negativity ASAP? Finding positive people who have lived through adversity and have a better life to show for it is a reminder that the past is not your present, you are worth forgiveness, you can achieve your goals, and you can become a positive force for others who need it.

Work It!

There are many techniques within the realm of positive psychology that have been shown to help increase hope and happiness in people who struggle. One technique is to reframe how we look at the everyday "mundane" activities or details of our lives. It is an obstacle to be bogged down by the negative idea that we are stuck. Can we learn to see the old ways as new again? Is there a way to stop taking for granted the gifts of our ordinary days? Try creating a time capsule with this exercise, adapted from a tool created by Elaine Houston:

The goal is to create a time capsule to rediscover the joy and unexpected benefits of ordinary, everyday experiences. Anyone who has looked at an old photo and said to themselves "I didn't realize how good I had it then" will see the power in this tool.

1. Use a notebook, scrapbook, pen, and paper or store your time capsule digitally—whichever method works for you.

2. Spend no less than thirty minutes to document ordinary daily experiences. A log of every single experience or detail is not necessary; however a good sampling of the essence of your daily life is recommended. Use sensory details, like smells, sights, and sounds, and include a range of experiences.
3. Store the time capsule out of sight, and set a reminder to revisit it in three months.
4. Notice if you smile or feel lighter remembering something you recorded. Maybe it was what seemed like an obligatory meeting, a botched recipe, or the repetitive task of putting the kids to bed. You might see that, in retrospect, you feel incredible gratitude for the moments that once appeared to be mundane.

Get Familiar with the Family Program

Historically, research has focused on measuring treatment outcomes on individual-based interventions, meaning that the family was not part of treatment. In addition, the recovery environment, a.k.a. relationship complications (such as angry parents or a spouse that uses drugs or alcohol), were not part of the continued care planning process. Patients would often go right back to the drama and chaos of their pretreatment lives because they were the only ones who changed. More recently, treatment programs have begun to expand treatment services to include family education and multifamily groups.

When looking at treatment options, you will want to explore and understand what is offered through a family program. Some outpatient programs will offer family education services. Residential treatment is where the most robust family programs will be found. The following are the main components and key considerations for family programs:

- *Family education* are psychoeducational groups that are offered in a lecture setting with other families. These lectures offer information on key topics that are relevant to your loved one's care and are helpful so that you speak the same language. If a new graduate from treatment returns home talking about their boundaries and post-acute withdrawals, we want it to be a source of comfort, not concern.

I have highlighted a few topics that are important tools for a loved one to have in understanding the disease of addition and other key components (communication, boundaries, and so on).

- Disease model of addiction: This explores why addiction is a chronic brain disease.
- Neurobiology of trauma: This demystifies trauma and the nervous system as well as explains behaviors (such as fight, flight, and freeze).
- Post-acute withdrawal: This informs us on what happens when acute detox is over and discomfort continues.
- Healthy communication: This teaches the proper use of "I" statements and boundaries.

- Family roles: This identifies how we take on roles to survive when navigating substance use disorder.
- Enabling: This defines and exposes how not to do things for our loved ones that they can do for themselves.
- Support groups: This connects us with other folks in a similar situation for connecting and understanding.

Once you understand the content, it's important that you make sure that the format works for you. The following are key factors:

Duration and delivery

- Live, virtual, or combo?
- How many days is it? (Most are between two and four days.)
- What are the living accommodations during the program?
- Is there any financial support if unable to pay for the hotel?
- Is the program on site or off site?
- Multifamily
    - Provides group therapy and lectures with other family members (This may or may not include your loved one in treatment.)
- One-on-one sessions
    - This is therapy that is conducted with either primary or family therapists and your loved ones. This gives you the opportunity to share your feelings.
- Continued care planning

- As we have discussed, creating a solid plan for continued care is essential for success. Having loved ones involved in the process can be extremely helpful in gaining buy-in on both an emotional and financial perspective. No surprises! For example, if someone is leaving residential, does the family support a sober living and partial hospitalization program, or if someone is stepping down from outpatient services, does the family want them to continue with a recovery coach or sobriety monitoring? Even details regarding expectations on job and finances can be sorted out in advance by having the family involved.

Play 2. Learn to Direct Drama

When a big change occurs in families, individuals tend to take on roles to help maintain functioning—even if it's dysfunctional. There is a central figure (often the identified patient), around whom others adapt their behaviors and reactions. Life seems chaotic, unpredictable, and sometimes frightening. Chaos can be addictive and so can assigning the identified patient the role of "the problem of the family." Family members will take on roles within the family, or sometimes even a mixture of roles, beyond the actual role they might have assigned themselves or have been assigned. Caregivers can become aggressors, partners can become victims, children can become caretakers, and so on. This changing of roles is often explained by a concept called the Karpman Drama Triangle.

The Karpman Drama Triangle, also referred to as "the victim triangle," was first put forth by psychologist Stephen Karpman in the late 1960s and has since been adopted as common use in counseling, therapy, and other fields. The model describes a common pattern of behavior in interpersonal relationships, particularly in situations of conflict or emotional turmoil. Understanding the three roles that make up the Drama Triangle, being aware of when you are assuming one of the roles, and knowing how to let go of the triangle are important parts of family healing.

The Drama Triangle places us in one of three roles that are interchangeable over time: victim, persecutor, and rescuer. The dynamic of assuming roles and playing different ones is a Karpman concept called "the game."

The payoff is different depending on which role we assume. Being a victim feels much different than being a rescuer. When someone is a victim, they passively wait for someone to come to their rescue, becoming childlike in their behavior. The rescuer, on the other hand, rides in on their white horse and plays hero. The child and the hero are very different roles but both are getting something out of it. Usually that something is avoiding a consequence or reality.

It is interesting that we all change places on the triangle depending on the circumstances and payoffs. I have seen many victims turn into persecutors when they don't get their way, and rescuers turn into victims when they feel unappreciated. Everyone has a preferred starting point, or where you hop on the triangle. Once you are in the triangle, like it or not, eventually you will be driven by guilt and fear to play all the roles.

The Victim

Victims believe that they are helpless and hopeless. Those in the victim role deny responsibility for their negative circumstances and deny possession of the power to change them. They use catastrophic language ("If you leave me, I'll never get better, and life won't be worth living," or "If I fail this test, my future is over.") and believe that "everyone" is doing "it" to them.

Victims look for a rescuer and believe that they need someone to take care of them, but instead of asking for help, they use blame and guilt to manipulate them into giving them what they need. Usually enabling happens due to this dynamic. The victim position is the key role in the triangle because it is the position the other roles revolve around.

The Rescuer

Rescuers step in to save or protect the victim. They may feel responsible for the victim's well-being and are constantly applying short-term repairs to a victim's problems, while neglecting their own needs. They work hard to help other people. They are harried, tired, and often have physical complaints. Whether they are a loud or quiet martyr, rescuers are angry and resentful underneath their outer shell of heroism. They are often criticized by the persecutor, with no recognition of any of their positive contributions. They, too, use guilt toward the victim to get their way and often have expectations of "repayment." Sometimes when these expectations aren't met, the rescuer can move into the victim or perpetrator role.

The Persecutor

The persecutor is the person or force that the victim blames for their problems. They are often seen as aggressive, dominating, or abusive. They often blame the victims and criticize the enabling behavior of rescuers, without providing guidance, assistance, or a solution to the underlying problem. Persecutors are critical, unpleasant, and good at finding fault. Underneath, they can feel inadequate. They gain control using threats, order, withholding (love, resources, and/or attention), and rigidity. Loud or quiet in style, persecutors can resemble a bully.

What's the motivation?

When we are in the triangle, we act out of fear. All three of the roles give us the illusion of

- power,
- safety/security,
- self-worth,
- connection, and
- trust.

The Drama Triangle concept can be invaluable in developing insight into our own family dynamics. You can explore the concept with or without your family. The key is self-awareness and owning your part and role. With this awareness, you become empowered to change your approach, and may soon find yourself developing empathy and compassion for others.

As you grow in self-awareness, watch out for enabling behaviors. As we have discussed, enabling this is usually the behavior of a rescuer. It is not uncommon for patients to realize through treatment that they have an enabler and call it out during treatment to work on it as a family. This is another reason identifying roles is critical to all members' healing.

How to get off the Drama Triangle:

- Be mindful of your motives. (What am I getting out of this?)
- Be mindful of your expectations. (What I am I expecting from others?)
- Stop blaming others—"I" statements help with this.
- Nurture yourself.
- Learn to set boundaries.

Am I Enabling?

According to the American Psychological Association, enabling is "a process whereby someone (i.e., the enabler) contributes to continued maladaptive or pathological behavior (e.g., child abuse, substance abuse) in another person." Or doing something for someone that they could do for themselves.

The enabler is typically a loved one or good friend who passively permits or unknowingly encourages unhealthy behavior in the other person. Enabling behaviors become dangerous when they are used as a roadblock to treatment. Enabling behavior can range from pretending there isn't a problem, to providing money to your loved one for drugs or alcohol, to taking on their responsibilities.

Common examples of enabling behaviors:

- Making excuses for the person
- Taking over their personal responsibilities

- Saving them from the consequences of their actions by fixing their problems
- Ignoring the problem or downplaying the severity (a.k.a. denial)
- Allowing substance use
- Keeping secrets
- Having an unrealistic view of family loyalty

Circle of Support

A family that I had been working with for quite some time walked into my office in a huff. Arms folded. Clinched jaws. Dad and Son sat together on the couch, and Mom sat by herself. This was most unusual for them. I asked what was going on. Son shared that they were not speaking to each other over the decision of when he (who recently was out of treatment) would get his motocross bike back. Mom wanted the bike sold. Dad wanted Son to get the bike back today. Son was triggered by his parents fighting about him (flashbacks to his childhood) and threatening to use. We had worked with the Drama Triangle in the treatment, and I asked them if they could see how it was playing out. They didn't see it so I assigned the obvious roles immediately as:

Mom: Persecutor
Dad: Rescuer
Son: Victim

This dynamic was uncomfortable for them as Dad was usually persecutor. Interestingly, Son was always victim, threatening to use, and he knew it. So, I shook it up showing Mom as the victim and reframed Dad as the perp who was manipulating to get closer to his Son and shove Mom out. Son didn't like this and came to the rescue of Dad. Seeing Son as the rescuer shifted the dynamic enough to shine a light on the fact that Son had gotten involved in his parents' issues too frequently throughout his childhood. We worked on him being empowered to say that he did not want to be in the middle of their marriage as victim or rescuer. He loved them both and did not want to be manipulated.

Play 3. Find a Support Group

Many support groups exist in every region of the United States and around the world to help family members and friends of those who have an addiction. You do not need to wait for a loved one to go into treatment. These groups provide education and information to help guide families through the process and can also offer support networks. The following are several options:

Al-Anon	A worldwide support group for family members and friends of those who are addicted to alcohol.
Alateen	A division of Al-Anon that is specifically designed for adolescent family members of alcoholics.
Nar-Anon	A worldwide support group for family members and friends of those who are addicted to drugs.

Narateen	A division of Nar-Anon that is specifically designed for adolescent family members of those who are addicted to drugs.
Families Anonymous	A group for relatives and friends concerned about the use of drugs or related behavioral problems.
GRASP	Grief Recovery After Substance Passing (GRASP) is a support group for people who have lost a loved one due to substance abuse.
NAMI	The National Alliance on Mental Illness (NAMI) provides a wide range of support options for loved ones of people suffering from symptoms of a mental health condition.
PAL	Parents of Addicted Loved Ones (PAL) is a Christian-based group of parents who help other parents learn how to cope with an addicted child and that allows for both educational and peer-sharing opportunities.
SMART Recovery	An alternative to Al-Anon that is science based and secular and provides tools for emotional support and coping.

Play 4. Set Boundaries

No doubt, while you are receiving education and support as a family member, the discussion of boundaries and boundary-setting will be explored. This is because so often, as we move through the roles in the Drama Triangle, we lose sight of our privacy, right to self-protection, and our own self-interest.

"As we move through the roles in the Drama Triangle, we lose sight of our privacy, right to self-protection, and our own self-interest."

What is a boundary? A boundary is something that we do for ourselves to set a border or limit. Boundaries can be physical, emotional, intellectual, or spiritual and spoken or unspoken; however, they should always be set as a way to take care of ourselves. A spoken boundary is one we set with others, and an unspoken boundary is one we set with ourselves regarding our *own* behavior.

Why Do We Lose Sight of Personal Boundaries?

Many experts have posited a few different reasons, some of which include the following:

- Our own trauma or past experiences/relationships can impact our ability to set and maintain healthy boundaries.
- A lack of self-confidence or self-worth will make us hesitant to put our needs first.
- Not being able to say no, a.k.a. people-pleasing, is a big one.

- Being passive in our communication makes our needs seem less important and signals to another that we might be boundaryless.
- Fear of abandonment as a result of you not doing something for someone or saying yes.
- Some cultures or communities expect certain actions and are more rigid about conforming or looking out for one's own needs first.

Not all boundaries look the same and may be adjusted based on the person you are interacting with. Boundaries can be fluid because their level of rigidity is related to how safe a person feels. If you feel secure, seen, heard, and/or validated in your relationship, then likely you will have fewer or less strict boundaries and display more vulnerability and intimacy. On the other hand, in cases such as with a history of physical or emotional abuse, people usually draw hard lines in the sand. Further, if someone has not earned your trust or has broken it, you might be more guarded and private about what you disclose or share.

While it's beyond the scope of this book to help you do the work to create and sustain boundaries, one technique is to create statements of self-talk that empower you and remind you that you have every right to your personal space and that your boundaries should never be crossed if you don't want them to be.

Work It!

Try these boundary statements or create your own. Note: You don't have to be in a toxic relationship or in the midst of a Drama Triangle to set boundaries. We all could use them.

- I am responsible for my own thoughts, feelings, and actions, and others are responsible for theirs.
- I give myself permission to set limits with others regarding their behaviors that affect me.
- Others have my permission to set limits with me about my behavior that affects them.

We set boundaries to take of care ourselves, *not* to control, manipulate, or change others' behaviors.

Format for Setting Verbal Boundaries with Others

Imagine the person you want to set boundaries with and acknowledge why this boundary is required.

Then write a statement specifying their action and your response.

Example: "If you, Dad, verbally abuse me by calling me a loser or a disappointment, I will end the conversation and talk to you later."

If you ______________________________

(insert specific behavior)______________________

____,

I will confront the behavior and share my feelings.

If you continue that behavior, to take care of
myself I will ________________________________
(insert personal plan of action)____________________
____.

So many family members don't have the words to communicate their boundaries to their loved ones. When leading a family program, I would give out copies of the following statements, which also hung in my office:

> I promise to support you with all of my love and available resources in every decision that is consistent with your health and life.
>
> I will not support you or provide any resources, financial or emotional, for any decision that may compromise your health, feed misery, and lead to your death. —*Anon*

I encouraged the families to take these statements home and even put them on their fridge. One day, I was referred to a client who had also gone through our treatment center. He looked at my wall and said, "Not that damn thing. It turned my mom into a monster, and I couldn't get away with anything anymore."

Mission accomplished.

CHAPTER 9

GO-TIME!

The Plays Upon Arrival to Treatment

"Sometimes when in a dark place you think you've been buried, when actually you've been planted."

—CHRISTINE CAINE

If you have turned to this chapter, you or your loved one have made the decision to go to treatment. Congratulations! You have gone through the financial arrangements, sorted through your insurance benefits, and weighed all of your options—macro and micro—for treatment programs. You might even have some tools now to understand each family dynamic better. When you have made the decision on where you will go, there are several important steps to take. (I encourage you to ask a trusted friend or family member to support you in sorting through these details.)

Some patients arrive for treatment in a nice vehicle, driven by a kind transport worker that has been hired by their treatment center. Others have a sad goodbye with a loved one who drops them off and reminds them how proud they are. These patients are often greeted by beautiful landscapes, wrought iron gates, signs of encouragement, and welcoming staff. Other folks are dropped off by law enforcement and arrive for treatment in handcuffs. Regardless of how the journey begins when someone walks in the door, hope is a companion. Research conducted by Nora Walker, MD, tells us that court-mandated treatment is often as effective as that of someone who seeks treatment on their own. Anecdotally speaking, I know this to be true. Some of the most motivated patients I have treated were licensed professionals themselves, like doctors, lawyers, and certified public accountants, with multiple DUIs, who were mandated by their licensing boards or by the court to attend treatment. These patients had everything to lose and no idea how to change. That is, until they arrived at treatment.

Regardless of whether it's hospitalized detox, residential treatment, or outpatient, the initial "drop off" has been known to induce many different emotions and scenarios. Second thoughts and self-doubt abound. Overwhelming sadness, anger, a desire to use, and even the compulsion to literally run away are not out of the ordinary. Know now that feeling any of these things is normal but is not a reason to exit. I want to set you up for success from the moment you step into the vehicle to treatment and the best way to do that is to give you a sneak peek as to what will greet you upon arrival. While the plays in this chapter mostly focus on residential treatment, they are relevant to any other treatment choice you've made because you'll understand the mindset and goals of your support staff and will be feel less defensive or ganged up on. You are not being punished, even though you might feel that way. This chapter pulls away the curtain, so you can see there is a method behind the mindset! If you know the expectations and rules and why they've been designed the way they have been, you will not feel blindsided or tricked. Positivity and collaboration with the process and the people will support your experience.

I have heard stories far too many times of people panicking and saying, "I can't do this" or "I'm out of here." Knowing exactly what is going to happen during the high-risk time, usually the first twenty-four to forty-eight hours, is essential to combat this fight-or-flight response. Any surprise might serve as an excuse to exit. What follows are the plays to best help you put one foot in front of the other, no matter how scary or dreadful it might feel, and enter those doors with hope by your side. Knowing that you can't bring a burner phone or vibrator and that you won't have endless access to your Instagram is essential.

"Positivity and collaboration with the process and the people will support your experience."

Play 1. Pack for Preparedness

Most programs will provide you with a list of what to bring and what not to bring. Some of the items are not as obvious or intuitive as you might think.

Practical Items

The American Addiction Center website's article "What to Bring to Rehab" presents a list of practical items that you can look over to help you prepare. This list is also an accurate reflection of the policies of most treatment centers. The text in brackets are my additions.

Each treatment center has different polices, and some are stricter than others. For the most part, it's recommended to pack the following:

- A list of names, addresses and phone numbers of those you need to communicate with during treatment. (Loved ones, healthcare professionals, 12-step sponsors, business contacts, and so on. Remember, you may have limited access to your phone to find this contact information.)
- Jewelry that you wear every day and consider to be a necessity [and provide a function], like your wedding ring or a watch. Otherwise, leave valuable [and sentimental] items at home.
- Your current prescription medication in the original pharmacy bottle with the information label intact. You should also bring a list of all your medications and dosages [for review].
- A small amount of cash (Ask your admissions coordinator what is recommended in terms of amount. Any larger amounts will most likely be placed in a safe to avoid misplacing it.]
- Your checkbook, credit card, or debit card to pay for incidentals [if required].
- Your insurance cards and a form of identification (driver's license, passport, [work permit], etc.). A valid form of identification is a requirement for most treatment centers.

- A calling card (if your facility requires them for long distance phone calls).
- Your rehab will likely provide reading materials for you. If you want to bring your own, they're usually required to be [books in the category of] recovery, self-help, or spirituality.

Clothing

Consider the season and weather of your treatment locale, and what outdoor activities will be available to you. These factors will impact your decisions on what clothes to pack. Here are recommendations from the American Addiction Center article that accurately represent the policies of most treatment programs that I have experienced:

> Most rehabs have a very strict dress code, so be aware of any restrictions while you're packing. If you're unsure about how to pack for the weather, pack layering options, like T-shirts, sweaters, cardigans and jackets. Keep in mind, space in your room may be limited, so try not to overpack.
>
> You will have access to a laundry machine at your center, so a week's worth of clothing should be enough. Be sure to pack clothes that are easy to wash.
>
> Bring seven days' worth of comfortable, weather-appropriate clothing. [Consider avoiding white, as there may be a rule about translucent

clothing, and white can get tricky. Also to be safe, it is best to choose shirts that don't have any symbols or sayings on them or sports teams and other affiliations. When in doubt, solid colors with no graphics. Some programs do not allow yoga pants or leggings unless you have a longer shirt that covers your back side] It is recommended that you ask for a packing list and dress code from your admissions representative and check your program's website for detailed information.

Personal Hygiene/Cosmetics

All items must be alcohol and propellant-free (non-aerosol) and must be in factory bottles with labeling. Travel bottles with no labels are prohibited. Most centers recommend that you bring thirty day's worth of essential products such as deodorant, toothbrush/toothpaste, haircare products, lotion and sunscreen. Please keep in mind that makeup and skin care will need to be alcohol free.

Other Items (Depending on the age requirement in state)

- iPods and MP3 players may be allowed (without a camera or internet function) at the designated time for exercise and sleep.
- Over-the-counter medications or supplements may be allowed but will need approval and arrive in unopened packages.

- Stuffed animals: In some programs they are not allowed due to hygiene but will have them available for purchase. Please clarify with admissions.
- Disposable razor or electric razor. Please clarify with admissions.

Contraband Items

All treatment programs prohibit certain items and will strictly enforce their polices by confiscating unapproved "contraband" items. They do so to ensure patient safety and to create a supportive recovery environment. The following items are most commonly against the rules:

- Drugs and/or alcohol: All medications are given to the medical department upon admission
- Pornographic material, adult toys, intimate products, or any similarly related item
- Toiletries and/or cosmetics that contain alcohol

Tobacco products

Use of cigarettes, tobacco, and vapes is another controversial topic in the operation of treatment programs. In a perfect world, treatment programs would be tobacco free, and patients enrolled in smoking cessation classes, along with all of their other programming. Our world is far from perfect, and my view of tobacco and tobacco-related products is harm reduction. Remember the advice about treating the alligator closest to the boat? It fits with tobacco. Asking someone to give up with tobacco along with their other drug of choice may be too much and serve as a barrier to treatment. On the other hand, some programs have a culture of smoking and even non-smokers start because the smoking area is the place to be in between groups. Programs will handle this issue in a variety of ways. The following are some highlights of the various approaches when navigating the process when you are searching for treatment. (Keep in mind that some states do not allow smoking until age twenty-one, and programs enforce this as best they can.)

- Cigarettes: Most will allow you to bring unopened packs of cigarettes, and there are also coordinated ways to safely purchase them. Families will often bring cigarettes when they visit or send them in a package.
- Chewing tobacco: Many do not allow chewing tobacco because of the mess. If your program does allow it, you will be asked to bring it in unopened packages.
- Vaping and e-cigarettes: Many programs will allow non-refillable/disposable e-cigarette products to be brought in unopened packaging, while others do not allow them at all.

- Any outside food or drink, even if in its original package and unopened.
- Weapons of any kind
- Magazines
- Video games or systems
- DVDs
- Candles and/or air fresheners
- Nail polish and remover
- Clothing that makes reference to drugs and/or alcohol, gang affiliation, or is sexually explicit in anyway or advertises sports teams.

You may be puzzled by the policies prohibiting sports teams. Many fans are quite spirited about their teams and players, so avoiding comments and arguments prompted by team wear has been adopted as best practice (especially around the World Series or Super Bowl time).

Most treatment centers will prohibit, or limit outside food and beverages. This is because many centers moderate sugar and caffeine intake and focus on a nutrition reset, where meals and snacks are carefully planned with the support of a dietician. If you have special dietary needs, such as Kosher meals or vegan, it is a good idea to discuss your program before you're admitted ensuring that your needs can be met.

If you arrive at your center and you find that you have packed something that is not allowed, most programs will store the items for you until you leave. If they will not store them, ask if they'll ship them home for you.

If you find that you need or want something else, most programs allow package delivery, within reason and within their own parameters. You may expect your package to be reviewed by staff while you open it. Your family and friends will most likely be able to send you packages as well, which will also be reviewed by staff. When family visits you, they will be required to sign in, and may be asked to leave their bags at the desk. If there is a safety concern (drugs, alcohol, or weapons), family members' bags may be searched as well.

Work It!

Schedule your admission. Time is of the essence when you agree to go to treatment. The goal wherever I have worked is to arrive within twenty-four hours from when the contract is signed for agreement to admission. This, of course, is if your admission is non-emergency. If you are in an emergency, a hospital is a better choice for you.

Ask your admissions representative about the best time of day for admissions. In my experience, it's during normal business hours when most of the staff is available. If you are scheduled for a weekend admission, ask what staff is available. Some programs have fewer staff on-site during the weekends. If it's going to be a few days before you meet your therapist, you want that expectation set to avoid disappointment. You will also want to know what your weekend programming will be like. Admitting to treatment and then having two days with nothing to do can put you into the flight stage and talk yourself into leaving. Many centers have robust weekend schedules, and you will be fine; it's just worth your peace of mind to ask.

Play 2. Be Clear on the Physical Admission Process

You are entering the no-judgment zone from the driver to the nurse to the therapist to the physician. This is our chosen work, and we do it because we know that you have a chronic disease, and we want you to heal. Speak the truth. No judgment here.

Addiction treatment centers vary; however, there are a few things that you should be prepared for when you get there.

Transportation

How are you getting to treatment? If you are driving yourself and have a vehicle, find out if it's okay to leave your car in the parking lot. If you are concerned about anything in the vehicle (drugs, alcohol, and/or weapons), please disclose this up front so that the program can assist you in either disposing or storing the item(s).

If you are flying, don't fly alone. Too many patients take a detour to the airport lounge, and we don't find them for a few days. Ask a friend or family member to go with you. If this isn't an option, ask the program if they can recommend or provide someone. There are wonderful services that offer trained professionals who can escort you safely to your destination. A warm introduction to the treatment center staff is always the goal.

Be sure that you have told the treatment center when your last drink was and coordinate the plan on preventing withdrawals. Again, it's best not to travel alone. Flight attendants are treatment savvy, so if you or your loved one tells a flight attendant that you are headed for treatment, they will not serve you alcohol—even if you ask.

When you land, the treatment center driver will most often be in the baggage claim area waiting for you. There are always discreet ways to identify each other; they won't have a sign. It's best practice to provide the treatment center driver with your cell phone and call them the minute you land. They can time you and will even talk with you as you walk past airport lounges. Treatment center drivers are usually in recovery and are kind and gentle souls who you will never forget.

Intake

When you arrive at the treatment center, you will be greeted by the intake staff. Your luggage will be taken from you and checked in a separate room. This is done for your safety. Many patients bring drugs (a.k.a. their "stash") into treatment. Some people keep it at home, some hide it in their cars, and some try to get it past the treatment walls. Your disease wants reassurance that if you change your mind about the whole treatment thing, you have the drugs available. It is the treatment center's job to keep you safe and protect you both from yourself and from someone else's stash.

Your luggage will be unpacked and inventoried by staff upon admission. This will happen while you are starting your intake process. Most treatment centers will do a thorough inventory of your belongings to avoid any misunderstandings if something is misplaced. This is also for your benefit. If you prefer to be in the room when your luggage is inventoried, just ask to be present. I've never heard of anyone being turned down. For any of us, seeing our belongings touched by someone else is a privacy violation and can be triggering. Facing this reality with humility and believing that it's being done for our own good is asking a lot on day one.

The Physical Exam

You will receive a complete history and physical, which is your first introduction to your medical provider. This may include a skin check, looking for bruises or other signs of wound/infections. They will also do a pain assessment to understand any pain issues that may be limiting your ability to move or be present in treatment and comprehensive blood work that is consistent with your history. When they ask about your drug and alcohol use, including when your last use was, please do not minimize, fabricate, or leave out any drugs. As we said earlier, substance use disorder is a chronic disease that impacts the whole person—mind, body, and spirit. Gathering your physical information will only enhance your recovery and make for a more comfortable detox, if necessary. You will be asked about sexual behaviors and may be screened for STDs. This is done to understand any high-risk sexual behaviors and to ensure that you are being treated for anything that may impact your health and the health of potential partners.

As part of your history, physical, and admission bloodwork, a treatment plan will be developed, identifying any medical needs. Many treatment centers will schedule and transport you to a dentist appointment, eye appointment, or other specialized services. These are things that are often neglected before treatment and getting up to date on dental and vision, to name a few, will be part of your healing.

Psych-Social Assessment

The biopsychosocial looks at the patient holistically in three major categories of life—biology, psychology, and the social environment.

After your biological and psychological information has been collected, your therapist will spend a lot of time with you on the social aspects of your life. This is because changes in your environment can have an impact on your mental health, both positively and negatively. For example, relationship, legal, financial, and housing issues have a huge impact on someone's mental health and substance use disorder. Creating a support system and stable housing may become key areas of treatment focus.

Much of the psych-social information will be collected preadmission; however, this will be your first exposure to your therapist. It's important that you don't minimize or leave anything out. We understand that these conversations can be painful and the events hard to talk about. The information is gathered with one thing in mind—your healing.

During the history, physical, and psych-social assessment, please be aware that the providers are mandated reporters, meaning that if you disclose something that is a danger to yourself or others or describes the abuse of a child or vulnerable adult, they are mandated by law to act upon it. Specifically, if you say that you are actively suicidal with a plan or if you have a plan to kill someone, you will be asked to go voluntarily to a higher level of care. If you decline, you can be petitioned or involuntarily committed to a higher level of care. In most programs, the petitioning of a patient happens infrequently, as the patient is part of the decision to go to higher level of care

Play 3. Settle in to Your Room Assignment

After your intake process, you will be assigned a room. If in detox, you will have twenty-four-hour nursing coverage and daily visits with a medical provider. While you may be introduced to a therapist and program components, minimal therapeutic work takes place during detox. The main priority will be your comfort, and if you are able to attend some groups that will be ideal.

If you go directly to residential treatment or after detox completion, you will be escorted to your room by a behavioral health tech. Most programs have roommates, and that is done for a few reasons. First, isolation is a huge trigger for folks in early recovery and having someone else who is going through the same thing while sharing the same space can be life changing. Not only does it build your recovery community, but it also allows you to practice compromise, healthy communication, and sensitivity to someone else's needs.

Most programs will get a good sense of roommate preferences and take great care to assign them appropriately. For example, someone who snores would not be placed with someone who is a light sleeper. Your roommate does not have to be your best friend; however, everyone deserves to feel safe and comfortable in their space. If you find your roommate triggering for whatever reason, (for example, if they remind you of an old coach that yelled at you), let the staff know immediately. There may be ways to work through the feelings with your therapist; however, moving rooms is most often an option.

You will be provided a program overview with a daily schedule. Our next chapter will review the treatment modalities, schedules, and what to expect on a daily basis.

Circle of Support

When I think about the experience of arriving for treatment, I think about my client Tabitha:

Tabitha agreed to go to treatment. She was scared and needed a way out of her present situation, but she was going to lay down some rules first. *Yup, time to take control.* "I don't want to be with any drug addicts, I'm going someplace warm, and I'm going to need a credit card for new summer clothes."

The admissions counselor told her what to expect upon arrival: She might have a roommate and they could accommodate her vegan diet. He had also been to treatment at the same program. This helped.

As they drove up the driveway to the treatment center and the gate opened, Tabitha felt a wave of terror. *Damn.* She needed her wine right now. She already needed vodka to get to sleep.

The nurse welcomed Tabitha and took her vitals, informing her that she needed to stay in detox for a few days. There she would meet her doctor and therapist. The tech went through her luggage. *What if he finds my pills, my burner phone, my vibrator?* Tabitha screamed in panic and shame. Too late—he found all three and confiscated them, storing them safely as "contraband."

Am I in prison? Every time she asked for something, like when she could use her phone or order something from Amazon, she was told she would have to talk to her team. "*What the hell does that mean—I have a team—is this a sport?* (She was not far off the mark. There was, in fact, a team in place to support her every step of the way,)

When Tabitha got to her accommodations at the lodge, she was greeted by other residents. *Inmates.* They told her she needed to wear a pink bike helmet so she wouldn't hurt herself while traveling to meetings in the "druggie buggy." For an instant, she believed them, but they burst out laughing and said, "Welcome to the nut house." Tabitha felt her body start to relax. They were warm and welcoming and soon to become her best friends for the next thirty days and beyond. Together, they made the decision to continue their treatment on an outpatient basis with sober living out of state and saw each other regularly at alumni events.

It did not take long for Tabitha to discover the power of the team. These were the people who would sit up with her all night when she was scared, listen to her deepest secrets, and help her look at herself in the mirror without self-hatred. They would even help her and her husband make amends so they might have a future together.

Looking back, Tabitha acknowledged, "This team gave me hope and helped me see my way out of the darkness so I could choose life, and I owe them my life. I can live with the shame of the choices I've made because I am worthy of life, love, and joy."

CHAPTER 10

TREATMENT COMPONENTS & DAILY SCHEDULE

The Plays for Working the Program

"The secret of change is to focus all your energy not on fighting the old but on building the new."

—DAN MILLMAN

Samuel entered residential treatment for the first time after believing for years that his drinking was something he could quit on his own. When his spouse left with the children, urging Samuel to seek treatment for his drinking and fits of anger and rage toward his young family, Samuel worked with his human resources manager to find a residential treatment that had the relevant treatment components for his individual needs. He needed a center close to home, so he could receive visits from his children, but also therapies that were trauma-informed, since he began to believe his turning to alcohol was related to adverse events in his childhood.

Upon entering the front doors of the center of his choice, he didn't know what to expect or how his day would be organized. He knew on some level there'd be therapy, and his cousin who was in recovery informed him about group sessions, but that was about all he knew. When Samuel received his welcome packet, his daily schedule looked something like this:

7:00 AM	Wake Up, Medications, Breakfast
8:00 AM	Goals Group "House Meeting"
8:30 AM	Exercise
9:30 AM	Process Group
11:00 AM	1:1 Therapy
12:00 PM	Lunch
1:00 PM	Lecture (Evidence-Based)
2:30 PM	Experiential, Bodyworks
4:00 PM	Lecture (Evidence-Based) or Medical Provider Visit
5:00 PM	Dinner
6:00 PM	Support Group Meeting (12-Step or SMART)
7:00 PM	Assignment Time or Exercise
8:00 PM	Healthy Electronics (FaceTime family)
9:30 PM	House Meeting—Gratitude Group
10:00 PM	Lights Out

Samuel became a bit overwhelmed about how packed and regimented the schedule was. And there were words he didn't understand, like "evidence-based," "experiential," and "SMART." Hour after hour, each event represents what is called a "treatment component" that he would engage in, each one having a specific purpose and goal. Even meal times are designed to be a meaningful part of the rehabilitation journey.

The various elements, strategies, or interventions in Samuel's schedule represent components that make up a comprehensive treatment program. To be considered comprehensive, the components holistically address the physical, psychological, and social aspects of substance use disorder and support long-term recovery.

As Samuel studied his schedule, he saw things that seemed up his alley, while others, like one-on-one therapy, made him a bit more apprehensive. Some seemed to have strengths and others had weaknesses, and he figured some things would be better for other people and not for him. But he wouldn't be able to skip anything. He made a note to discuss individualizing his day more when he met with his therapist now that he had a handle on how his day would flow.

The purpose of this chapter, and the plays within it, is to break down each of the treatment components that will fill up your daily schedule and demystify things like "SMART," "experiential" and "evidence-based" therapies. By becoming acquainted with the various modalities before you enter rehab, whether residential or otherwise, you will be armed with information to make informed decisions, tailor your treatment plan, and amplify your experience. The goal is to finish what you start, and even a baseline understanding of what your team will be helping you accomplish day after day will increase the likelihood of graduating.

Play 1. Work with Evidence-Based Therapies

As you were weighing your options and exploring programs that fit your needs, you likely came across the term "evidence-based" to describe treatment modalities, from therapy to detox to medications. Evidence-based means what it sounds like: there is data and scientific evidence that the modality had been effective in treating substance use disorder. These therapies have undergone rigorous testing and evaluation to determine their effectiveness in treating substance abuse.

The main benefit of evidence-based therapies is that they provide a roadmap to recovery that is substantiated by research, personalizing the path for each individual while utilizing techniques that have been verified for their effectiveness. Because these therapies have been rigorously tested, they are more likely to result in lower relapse rates and improved quality of life over the long term.

Insurance companies require the use of evidence-based treatment, which is why programs create their daily structure using evidence-based components. If they don't meet these requirements, which is called "intensity of service," an insurance provider probably won't pay the rehab center. What this means to you is that you can expect a quality residential treatment center to deliver evidence-based therapies a minimum of six hours a day. The types of therapies will range vary from medication-assisted treatment to cognitive behavioral therapist and dialectical behavior therapy, depending on the training and expertise of staff. Take a closer look at Samuel's schedule, and you'll note therapies delivered via one-on-one sessions, small groups, and psychoeducation lectures, all of which are considered evidence based. Support groups, especially 12-step, are also considered evidence based and are an essential part of the healing process.

The following list is not meant to be all inclusive; however, it shows the evidence-based therapies that, in my experience, are frequently offered in treatment programs.

The National Association of Addiction Treatment Providers article on treatment methods provides the following summaries:

> *Individual Counseling:* By speaking with a licensed counselor on a one-on-one basis, a person in recovery can gain a better understanding of their addiction and the factors contributing to it. This approach is also called "talk therapy."
>
> *Group Counseling:* In group therapy, recovering individuals share their stories and learn from the experiences of others, decreasing feelings of loneliness and isolation common to active addiction. These meetings are sometimes called "process groups."
>
> *Cognitive Behavioral Therapy (CBT)* addresses the negative thought patterns and behaviors that lead to substance abuse. It equips individuals with coping mechanisms and problem-solving skills, aiming to prevent relapse....
>
> *Medication-Assisted Treatment (MAT)* is one of the most effective types of evidence-based therapy for addiction, particularly for treating opioid, alcohol, and nicotine addiction. It involves using medications alongside behavioral therapy to manage withdrawal symptoms and reduce cravings....

Dialectical Behavior Therapy (DBT) is often used for individuals with emotional regulation issues or borderline personality disorder alongside substance abuse [co-occurring disorders]. It teaches mindfulness, [distress tolerance], and emotional regulation skills to help manage stress and reduce dependence on substances....

Motivational Interviewing (MI) is a patient-centered approach designed to spark motivation to change. It focuses on resolving ambivalence to facilitate the stages of change [see chapter 2] and recovery.

MI is extremely effective for the treatment of addiction and the management of physical illnesses and ailments. Through MI, therapists inspire patients to alter behaviors that negatively impact their health. MI is ideal for addicted individuals who are unmotivated or unprepared for change (pre-contemplative stage).

MI works by encouraging people to work through their feelings about behavior change and to explore discrepancies between their current behavior and life goals. I have seen this work with young adults who were smoking marijuana daily and experimenting with opioids. I asked a former patient who was in his late twenties, whose life had been negatively changed by heroin use, to speak with the younger patient. He shared that his goal of playing baseball in college, even going to college, had been destroyed because he progressed from marijuana to Percocet and ultimately heroin. We asked the younger patient what his goals were and to visualize what he wanted his life to be in five years.

We all discussed how continuing to use drugs did not honor those goals.

Many treatment centers will utilize reward systems to reinforce positive behaviors. For example, I once implemented a phase system which increased privileges based on adherence to rules, assignment completion and group attendance (and timeliness). Privileges range from additional gym time to watching a sporting event. We found that one of the most valued privileges was the opportunity to sleep late on a Saturday. These reward systems are rooted in the concept of *Contingency Management*, another evidenced based behavioral therapy.

Experiential Therapies

Samuel was curious when he saw experiential therapies listed in his 2:30 time slot, but what did it mean? And would it be different each day?

The National Association of Addiction Treatment Providers article further describes experiential therapy as follows:

> "When most people picture addiction treatment, they think of traditional talk therapy: a series of conversations spread over several sessions. However, hands-on learning, [in which a person uses expressive tools and activities, such as guided imagery, role-playing, and art therapy,] can also be a powerful tool for those in early recovery. Experiential therapy is effective for the treatment of substance use disorders because it deeply engages the patient's emotions.

> Participants explore subconscious thoughts and feelings.... In this way, people who cannot articulate complex emotions (or convey the details of their trauma) [in traditional talk therapy may begin processing them]." Some experiential therapies are considered evidence based, and some are not.
>
> Examples of experiential therapy include:
>
> - Equine Therapy
> - Movie Therapy
> - Art therapy

There are also services offered at treatment centers that are most often not covered by insurance; however, they still have a meaningful impact on health and well-being—especially in early recovery. The following are examples:

- Massage
- Acupuncture
- Biofeedback/Neurofeedback
- Occupational therapy

Circle of Support

When we think of occupational therapy, we often think of hospital-based workers who teach people how to do the basics (hygiene, movement, and so on) after an illness, surgery, or injury. Occupational therapy can also be invaluable in early recovery and is offered at very few treatment centers. The main way that I have seen occupational therapy be effective is in sensory reprocessing—showing patients how to guide their senses to regulate their nervous systems. Sensory processing aims to inform people about why they are having physical symptoms of panic or fear. When your nervous system detects that you are in danger, it feels threatened and puts our bodies in a protective state of fight, flight, or freeze. So many people in treatment experience the phenomena of one or more of these responses and make poor decisions, whether it be to retreat and isolate, lash out at a team member, or leave treatment rashly. When someone understands that they have the capability to self-guide their senses back to a regulatory state, it can be incredibly empowering.

The patients at the program where I most recently worked spent time in sensory rooms. At first, they would walk in and say, "This is woo-woo shit," but within ten minutes they witnessed how swinging in a chair, being surrounded by calming hues of light and music, touching various textures, smelling soothing smells (lavender and peppermint), or eating a Warhead sour candy could interrupt a panic attack or calm them enough to do the next right thing, like ask for help.

It was such a gift to see these seemingly simple things have a huge impact on our patients, and everyone left treatment with their own "sensory kit." Occupational therapists also helped with the basics on sleep hygiene, pain management, and vocational goals; however, nothing was as magical as seeing the light go on with some when they realized the power that they had within their own senses.

Group Activity Attendance: "Why Do I Have to Go to Everything?"

Samuel was encouraged to attend all activities. He was told it was for his own good. This is so true, which is why you will hear the exact same thing when you receive your schedule and begin to experience the various treatment components discussed throughout this chapter.

Being able to follow a schedule and keep a commitment is an important first step toward recovery. I will never forget leading a group in a treatment center and a group member, Rusty, came in at the halfway point. Another resident in the group, Bill, asked Rusty to never do that again. Bill had presented his lifeline, and he wanted Rusty there. Rusty asked, "What do you care if I'm here?"

To which Bill said, "You might just say something that will save my life."

Beautiful. He was never late or missed group again, and I have recycled that line many times with the same impact.

Other reasons why attendance matters: For insurance to pay for your care, you need to attend the required number of hours or demonstrate "intensity of service." If the program can't document a reason for the absence (usually a medical excuse is required) and their efforts to get you to attend, they run the risk of not being paid for the day. There are some programs that have a policy that if they aren't paid and it is due to lack of attendance, they will bill you directly for the day.

The other reason for attendance is for safety. If you are not in the group where your schedule says you should be—where are you? Programs need to be able to account for everyone in real time for safety purposes. Patients are not meant to be alone in their room or wandering the parking lot instead of being in group. It is amazing to see one hundred-plus patients all be located and documented in less than ten minutes. That is quality care.

Play 2. Explore the Philosophy and Offerings of Support Groups

The Twelve Steps of Alcoholics Anonymous (aa.org)

1. We admitted we were powerless over alcohol—that our lives had become unmanageable.
2. Came to believe that a Power greater than ourselves could restore us to sanity.
3. Made a decision to turn our will and our lives over to the care of God *as we understood Him*.
4. Made a searching and fearless moral inventory of ourselves.
5. Admitted to God, to ourselves, and to another human being the exact nature of our wrongs.
6. Were entirely ready to have God remove all these defects of character.
7. Humbly asked Him to remove our shortcomings.
8. Made a list of all persons we had harmed, and became willing to make amends to them all.

9. Made direct amends to such people wherever possible, except when to do so would injure them or others.
10. Continued to take personal inventory and when we were wrong promptly admitted it.
11. Sought through prayer and meditation to improve our conscious contact with God *as we understood Him*, praying only for knowledge of His will for us and the power to carry that out.
12. Having had a spiritual awakening as the result of these steps, we tried to carry this message to alcoholics and to practice these principles in all our affairs.

Support groups provide a sense of community for those in recovery. There are a number of options when it comes to support groups, so keep trying them out until you find a good fit. In addition to the widely recognized 12-step programs with spiritual components, such as Alcoholics Anonymous, several secular groups promote abstinence as well, such as SMART Recovery. I have worked with hundreds of clients who say they can't do 12-step because they don't believe in God or have a higher power. I am not a 12-step expert by any means; however, when a person feels this way, I usually ask them to read steps one and two in the 12-steps before making a final decision.

- "Step one: Admit we are powerless over our addiction and our lives have become unmanageable."

  I ask, "Does that fit?"

"Yes" is usually the response.

- "Step two: Come to believe that a power greater than ourselves could restore us to sanity."

  Step two is usually when a person adamantly answers, "I don't believe in God."

  I ask back, "Do you think you are God?"

  "Well…no" is a common answer.

  "That's a start. Is anything bigger or more powerful than you that you can't see? The wind, love?"

  "Well, sure."

  That's another step in the right direction.

  "The wind can be your higher power for now," I say.

Just embracing that we are powerless and not in control is a great start. Regarding 12-step, the science tells us that it works, so it is considered evidence based. Second, the steps are a roadmap to life, humbly realizing that we are not all powerful and learning how to live with accountability, make amends when wrong, and seek support. It makes good sense for anyone.

The 12-Step Model

All 12-step groups are based on the principles set forth by Alcoholics Anonymous. They are spiritually based (higher power) programs providing support to members who are in recovery from substance, behavioral, and emotional addictions and codependency. The 12-steps refer to a suggested program for living that allows healing to occur.

The following is a list a 12-step programs. (Some have been mentioned in chapter 8, "Family Matters"):

- AA—Alcoholics Anonymous
- Al-Anon—Alcoholics Anonymous for family members
- CoDA—Co-Dependents Anonymous
- NA—Narcotics Anonymous
- SAA—Sex Addicts Anonymous
- EA—Emotions Anonymous
- RCA—Recovering Couples Anonymous
- ACA—Adult Children of Alcoholics
- Celebrate Recovery—based on Christian principles

Each of these programs is commonly offered in treatment programs, and you will be asked to "work the steps," which means actively engaging in and completing the twelve steps.

The following is an overview of the steps as described by the "Twelve-step program" Wikipedia article:

As summarized by the American Psychological Association (APA), the process involves the following:

- admitting that one cannot control one's alcoholism, addiction, or compulsion;
- coming to believe in a Higher Power that can give strength;
- examining past errors with the help of a sponsor (experienced member);
- making amends for these errors;
- learning to live a new life with a new code of behavior;
- helping others who suffer from the same alcoholism, addictions, or compulsions.

If you are working the steps while in treatment, you are supported by your therapist and/or other staff in recovery. If you work the steps outside of treatment, you don't work these steps alone; you typically work them with a sponsor.

A sponsor is an active member of a 12-step community whose role is to help new members interpret and develop a recovery program that will work for them based on their own experience. A sponsor guides the newcomer through the working of the steps.

Another popular and effective support group is Self-Management and Recovery Training Recovery, or SMART Recovery.

The SMART Recovery page "What is SMART Recovery?" describes the program as the following:

1. Build and maintain motivation
2. Cope with urges and cravings
3. Manage thoughts, feelings and behaviors
4. Live a balanced life

Both 12-step and SMART attempt to treat substance abuse, and both encourage group meetings, but they differ in several key areas, based on the SMART Recovery FAQ page.

12-Step	**SMART**	
Foundation:	Spiritual	Scientific
Teaching style:	Higher Power	Self Reliance
Meeting style:	Presenter Style	Discussion Style
Length:	Lifetime	Months or years
Sponsors:	Having one is a major tenet	No Sponsor
Language:	Admit Addiction	Discourages labels

Refuge Recovery

Refuge Recovery is a popular support group option that draws on Buddhist philosophy to help people who are coping with urges and other difficulties in sobriety. Much of the teachings in Refuge Recovery are based on the Buddhist philosophy that the root cause of suffering is people's desire to push away pain. The Refuge Recovery Program does not require anyone to subscribe to a specific belief. They do, however, ask that members trust the process and do the work necessary for recovery. Participants learn how drinking alcohol and using drugs keeps them stuck in suffering. Through mindfulness and other Buddhist practices they learn to have compassion for themselves and the pain they've experienced as well as develop healthy coping strategies to deal with triggers. Refuge Recovery is often popular with individuals who struggle with the belief in a higher power that is fundamental in the 12 Steps, however, I have seen Refuge Recovery work in conjunction with 12 Step and it doesn't have to be an either-or situation.

Certain treatment centers are known for their expertise in specific modalities. If a modality resonates with you, seek a treatment center whose therapists hold the proper credentials.

This is especially true where trauma is concerned. If a patient's life is a building, trauma is the fire in the basement. If not treated properly, the risk for relapse is high.

For Fans and Family

So many families worry about the social and community aspect that they are entrusting their loved one to. The vibe, the energy, and the examples of others in treatment can impact your loved one's attitude toward recovery. The "soul of the program" is something you probably learned about as you helped your loved one research treatment facilities. A program's "soul" refers to the unique culture, values, and atmosphere of a program or facility. These are the things you cannot see, like the passion and enthusiasm of a staff member or ceremonies and rituals, that add to the identity, efficacy, and client experience.

The soul is created by the history and legacy of the program. Treatment centers stand on sacred ground where lives were saved—and lives were lost—where families were reborn and marriages saved, where intern counselors grew in their levels of competence and confidence to become leaders. All these things are intangible and equally important to facilitate healing. Why? Because the energy of the program and the staff impact the patients. We become the container to hold their emotions and replicate the family structure. Some treatment centers are very good at recognizing that a sense of community and belonging are built through therapeutic communities by focusing on helping people develop new and healthier values, attitudes, and behaviors.

So often people who seek treatment are disenfranchised from their community and families, which is what precisely might worry fans and family members. With their self-esteem at its lowest, a person's ability to connect with a group and be a "part of" a healing community can make all the difference. Some centers even call the community a "tribe." I have seen therapeutic communities built in treatment, creating places to belong in myriad ways. Here are some of my favorites:

1. Daily morning and evening meetings in the house/lodge:

   The residents set an intention for the day, expressing gratitude and then review their daily schedule. If there are any scheduling issues, a healthy mechanism for resolution is available. There is a patient leader that is appointed by the other residents who leads the meeting. If there are any internal issues, they are discussed and handled at this time. The issues can be simple, like the residents wanting more puzzles, to more complex ones, like if a resident accuses another of stealing. The establishment of habits, such as engaging in healthy conflict resolutions, setting a daily goal, and expressing gratitude before the day begins, is a form of cognitive restructuring (replacing old or unhelpful thoughts and behaviors with positive ones) that once established can continue after treatment.

2. All-community meetings:

   These are typically held weekly or biweekly and are heavily attended by staff. I have seen them used for conflict resolution, acknowledgment and recognition, and communication of important events. The goal is healthy problem-solving and celebration with the support of the community.
3. Rituals and traditions:

   These are awarded for a variety of reasons to residents at varying stages of the program. Sometimes they are awarded by other residents, sometimes staff. For example, at one program, the "talking stick" was awarded to the resident who had emerged as a leader in the group.
4. Labyrinths:

   Labyrinths are ancient, sacred symbols that represent a journey or quest because they have a single path that leads to the center and back out again. They are not to be confused with mazes, which have many dead ends. Labyrinths can be a therapeutic tool because walking a labyrinth can represent the journey of recovery, with the twists and turns along the way. Many people find walking through a labyrinth to be a form of meditation, others consider it symbolic of the challenges of life and finding one's way to reach the exit.

5. Tributes:

   Tributes to former patients or staff who have passed away honor their spirit and remind us that life is short, and we are all connected as a recovery community.

6. Recreational activities:

   These are examples of activities practiced to remind patients that you can have fun, sober experiences that connect them to the community.

   a. Kickball (staff vs. patients)
   b. BBQs (weekly)
   c. Carnival games
   d. Talent shows

7. Motivational Speakers:

   Provide hope, inspiration and entertainment most often on weekends in community.

   a. Alumni
   b. Appropriate Comedians

The community, or "milieu" as we call it, takes on an energy or vibe of its own. Some can be very positive, supporting each other through the tough work. Others can be quite toxic, convincing patients that staff is "out to get them," the food is awful, and a myriad of other negative things that threaten a person's completion of treatment. Behaviors, both good and bad, become contagious. The program's soul is either uplifting or sabotaging. It's up to savvy treatment professionals to feed the good and learn from the bad—nipping it in the bud before there are negative consequences.

Play 3. Trauma Treatments

In chapter 4, which explored co-occurring disorders and the effect of trauma on a person with substance use disorder, we discussed the prevalence of adverse childhood experiences. Simply put, trauma creates dysregulation in our nervous system, and often substances are used as coping mechanisms when we experience the symptoms of fight, flight, or freeze. For example, some individuals may constantly feel angry, on edge and unable to settle—or nervous system activation. They may find themselves unable to be in a relationship with others, run away from conflict or engage in risky behaviors. (Fight or flight). Others may experience depression, low energy, lack of motivation, or freeze. The way that trauma shows up in our lives influences what substances we are drawn to that will provide the desired effect, which is to make the pain go away. Trauma treatment focuses on creating nervous system regulation and providing tools for an individual to self soothe and is often described as "top down" or "bottom up." A top-down trauma treatment focuses on cognitive processes, or your finding tools to manage your thoughts. Bottom-up trauma treatments work on where trauma shows up in your body and focuses on ways to regulate breathing and other sensory integration.

As you consider your choice of a treatment program, if you feel that your trauma needs to be addressed alongside your substance use disorder, it is recommended that you focus on programs with specific evidence-based treatment modalities. There are many trauma specialty programs with trained experts in effective modalities depending on what your specific needs may be.

Work It

Many programs are designed to reinforce healthy sleeping and eating habits and are built into the daily schedule to ensure as such. Weekends may be a bit lighter and account for family visits, and so on. The days and evenings are very busy. Some patients report having too much, while others will say that they are bored with any free time or options at all. This is where the individualized nature of the treatment plan comes in to play, as well as the collaboration with your therapist on tailoring evidence-based therapies appropriate to your needs. They will work with you to adjust your schedule, as long as you are meeting the "intensity of service" requirements.

Putting together all of the components discussed in this chapter will create the plan for your care. You will have a treatment plan that is individualized for your specific needs. This is required by regulatory agencies.

The individualized treatment plan will incorporate the following:

- Presenting problem
- Goals
- Progress on goals
- Clinical recommendations

It is important that you be an integral part of your treatment plan and that you receive regular updates on your progress. This is where your therapist's input is invaluable to planning the next steps in your care and making recommendations for continued areas of focus.

Being individualized and mindful of the modalities available to you and how they come together to form a holistic picture of treatment will help you continue your journey. There will be bumps in the road and things that arise that might threaten your commitment to treatment once you are there. With more information and preparation, we can ward off such things. We want to get you to graduation and sober living. Supporting treatment completion is the focus of the next chapter.

TEAM MEETING

Interview with Tena Moyer, MD

Jaime Vinck: What should someone look for in a treatment center?

TM: Before you start looking for a treatment center, you must start looking at what you really want out of the treatment center. So many people go into treatment because their families can't put up with their behavior anymore or because there's a legal problem. If the patient is really, really lucky, they come because they don't like living their life the way they've been living it. That means that it is their choice to be doing treatment rather than an externally imposed reason.

If you're going to choose to go into treatment, you have to understand that you are casting your life into a completely unanticipated, unimagined experience because we use our addictions, whether they're process addictions, like eating disorders or gambling, or sexual compulsivity or substance addictions, to manage our inner life.

In treatment, you're not going to have those things available to manage your inner life. What that means is [that] you have to view it not as a program of self-improvement but instead, the opportunity to experience yourself in a way you have not experienced yourself, maybe ever.

But certainly, as long as whatever addiction or behavior has been active, it's really hard to do because we develop those behaviors because they're protective. I mean, nobody blows out the candle on their birthday cake when they're ten and says, "I want to be an alcoholic when I grow up." Nobody does that. They want to be firemen or ballerinas. But somehow you ended up there. You chose those drugs or behaviors because at the time, they helped.

The real challenge of choosing treatment is to recognize that whatever helped before is harming now. That means [that] you have to be willing to feel the grief and the loss of the behavior. To feel the frustration of not being in control. *To be willing to allow the external world that is in a treatment center to structure your life rather than being the chaotic captain of your own life in addiction.*

I've heard from many patients [that] they're mad because they can't have their phones, or they can't have their social media time and they can't have snacks in their room and they have to keep their schedule. I really get it. I don't know if I would do well in a treatment center. The bottom line is [that] all of those parameters are in place so that you can focus on your addiction and whatever is troubling you—depression, grief, anxiety, etc.—and not use them as distractions, the way that you always have. That would be my advice to anybody looking at treatment. Unfortunately, a lot of people are limited in choice due to insurance considerations.

When I recommend people to a treatment center, I say is what treatment is not going to be. I want to be really clear here. Considering a program is not thinking, "What can I get away with and how will they let me have my phone?" It's how flexible they are in altering the treatment plan to meet who I am as a person.

It has nothing to do with having your cell phone.

What it does mean is that you choose a program where you feel seen and heard by your team, which may also mean [that] you feel angry and frustrated. Yet, you can believe that the team is truly supportive, even when they are frustrating. The team will frustrate you, no matter where you go.

JV: Do you have any final words that you'd like to share about being a psychiatrist, about our field, about being on a team?

TM: I can only say that when I quit medicine many years ago and switched to psychiatry, I just realized I hated getting up in the morning and doing my job. I realized it was a job and not a career, even though I like medicine. Now, I can truly say [that] I get up every morning and even on the days that I don't want to go to work; I'm really lucky to do what I do. I know that when I go to work, I am just going to be filled up by the people that I'm working with, whether they're my colleagues or my patients.

CHAPTER 11

GETTING TO THE FINISH LINE

The Plays for Completing Treatment

"You can't fail at recovery; you can only quit trying."

—UNKNOWN

Nothing in life takes a straight path. As mentioned, this is especially true in recovery, which is why walking a labyrinth on the grounds of some treatment centers is a popular component. With its twists and turns and challenges to find the exit point, the labyrinth is a metaphor for the time, energy, and mindfulness that it takes for a person to come out on the other side of substance use disorder.

This entire book has been about demystifying each part of the process you will undertake as you consider and enter rehabilitation, all because setting expectations before you go will help increase the likelihood of treatment completion. *This* is the end game—crossing the finish line. Doing so means that you can experience the benefits of the powerful treatment components discussed in the last chapter. The professionals in the addiction and recovery world focus on treatment completion not just because we want people to learn all the ways that can help them achieve their recovery goals, but because we know that completing a program results in a higher sobriety rate. According to the National Association of Addiction Treatment Providers Foundation of Recovery Science and Education, people who spend more than thirty days in treatment report lower post-treatment substance use and have an overall higher quality of life. Depending on the source, the overall treatment completion rate for residential treatment is somewhere in the vicinity of 70 percent. What this means is that for every ten people who seek treatment in a residential facility, *three* of them will leave early against medical advice (AMA). That's too high for my taste. Think about that compared to other chronic diseases. It's possible to think that a diabetes client may forget to take their medication or splurge on a dessert, but purposely quitting their treatment protocols against their doctor's advice?

When it comes to substance use disorder, people leave treatment prematurely, also known as "unplanned" discharges, more than any other chronic disease. Unplanned discharge prevents clients from completing their planned course of treatment and "intensity of care" that was designed specifically with their individualized treatment plan in mind. Early departures like these lead to increased risks of relapse or life-threatening health complications.

Just like there are a number of reasons a person might use to avoid entering treatment, there are a number of factors that contribute to a person leaving prematurely. My goal is to lay out the most common causes of premature discharge so you can overcome doubts, concerns, and overall trepidation that might lead you to second guessing treatment and leaving before you can reap the rewards.

Play 1. Be Aware of the Types of Unplanned Discharges, How Often They Occur, and a Program's Philosophy on Implementation

Not all unplanned discharges are due to a person choosing to go against the advice of their treatment team; however, AMA (a.k.a. ACA—against clinical advice) is the most pervasive type.

AMAs means a client opts to leave treatment before their treatment goals are met and without the approval of their treatment team. The percent of AMAs in a program can range anywhere from 5 percent to 25 percent, depending on a variety of factors.

Doing the work in treatment is hard. For many, it's the first time people admit to, dissect, and face their own trauma, which can cause a trauma response: fight, flight, or freeze. For those not doing specific trauma work, admissions of negative emotions such as shame, guilt, and fear can be overwhelming and feel defeating, causing them to question their worth or their own ability to overcome their substance use disorder. Regardless, when a client comes face-to-face with the hard stuff day in and day out and has to do so with clinicians, therapists, and other people just like them, they can become emotionally dysregulated. Please know now, this is common. It's also common to be triggered by something or someone seemingly unrelated to a trauma, causing us to want to run away from it, which comes in the form of leaving treatment. For instance, one of my clients in a one-on-one session recalled being bullied and beaten up by her classmates in sixth grade and that her parents and teachers failed to come to her defense. The session also led to my client admitting that she became a bully herself when she became an adult and did some regretful and shameful things. Session over.

The real fireworks happened after my client attended the group session later that day. A few of the residents confronted her regarding some aggressive bullish behaviors at rec earlier in the day—where they perceived she was being a bully. My client was immediately activated and looked at her team leader, asking, "Are you going to just let them do this?" The client left the group session triggered and, in a high state of activation, went to the desk and said, "Fuck it. I'm out."

For Fans and Family

If you believe that your loved one might be at risk of or prone to leaving AMA, there are many different approaches that you might expect to be taken if this occurs. Some are less desirable while others are more effective responses, which can explain the percentage range in AMA across programs:

1. Program says, "He's not ready for treatment; let him go" and calls him an Uber.
2. Tech at the desk tries to talk with him and asks him to go on a walk.

3. Tech at the desk finds another therapist (or leader) that is available to talk with him.
4. Tech uses other techniques to hit pause and regulate his emotions.
   - Walk
   - Mindfulness/Meditations
   - Sensory tools (oils, Warheads, fidget toys)
   - Remind them what life looked like *before* treatment
   - Remind them of their vision for their lives
5. Therapist calls family member or referent for support

"If you are called to speak to your loved one who is in an activated state and says that they want to discharge from treatment early, listen empathically, understand their concerns, and provide support."

If you are called to speak to your loved one who is in an activated state and says that they want to discharge from treatment early, listen empathically, understand their concerns, and provide support. Give your loved one the opportunity to voice why they want to leave and assuage your temptation to interrupt or sound judgmental. After you show them that you understand their perspective, validate their feelings. Letting them know you acknowledge their feelings and emotions can be powerful and calming. Let them know it's normal to experience challenges; you might remind them of this very chapter that openly discussed the reality of these kinds of moments occurring.

Reiterate to your loved one their "why" for entering treatment, articulate the progress they've made, even by simply walking through the door, and the potential ramifications of leaving prematurely. Encourage them to utilize their treatment team by discussing their concerns and find solutions before making a final decision. If they have a sensory room, encourage your loved one to utilize it. Finally, remind them that you are there to support them, and you are glad that they called you in this moment of challenge.

In programs that I run, anything in the double digits for AMA rates is unacceptable. I challenge the staff to think about what they would want a treatment team to do and/or say to their loved one who might be running out the door of treatment in a heightened state and to accept nothing less of their own words and actions.

We are not always successful in getting someone to change their mind about leaving treatment. I believe a best practice is to have them wait twenty-four hours before leaving. Distance from the heightened state can do wonders to reregulate the body's trauma response. Impulsivity can lead to dangerous decisions and getting that twenty-four-hour commitment is important.

Even if they still decide to discharge, at least with a day to settle down, they can properly plan next steps, consider their medications, secure safe transportations, and give their emotions a chance to regulate. Of course, we hope that they change their mind; however, even if they don't, they have practiced using the pause button.

I also believe it's best practice to have someone from the program reach out to the resident within twenty-four hours of their departure to check in. This call reminds the person that the program is still a safe, caring place. Often, the client will ask if they can return.

Administrative Discharges

When the treatment center discerns that a client should no longer remain at their facility, that is called an administrative discharge. These are disciplinary in nature and are typically for breaking rules that could impact client safety. Some examples are

- bringing drugs on property,
- sexual activity between clients, or
- violence toward staff or clients.

When interviewing treatment programs, it is helpful to find out the percentage of administrative discharges that are doled out each year. Again, anything in the double digits is alarming and could indicate a lack of organization and regimen on behalf of the professionals. In some cases, if action isn't taken to administratively discharge someone, other clients might feel unsafe or unfocused and opt to leave on their own, thereby increasing the AMA rate.

As professionals, we often discover that undesirable behaviors are symptoms of the disease, and punishing feels wrong.

Success with administrative discharges would be to transfer to another program. Setting boundaries is critical to show the other residents that we will keep them safe. Having a few programs close by for admin discharge transfers is important. When seeking out the right treatment center, add to your interview questions, "What happens to the client if they are administratively discharged?"

Medical Discharges

If it isn't known through the admissions process that someone has a medical condition that makes it impossible for them to participate fully in the program, a medical discharge is in the best interest of the client. Examples of this would be

- heart issues,
- seizures. or
- gastrointestinal issues.

Medical discharges are rare, and as we discussed in chapter 9, a comprehensive preadmission assessment can often help avoid this issue.

Transfer of Care

If, during the course of treatment, someone's condition worsens or new symptoms emerge, you may be transferred to another facility for safety reasons. Examples include

- active suicidal ideations with plan,
- active eating disorder behaviors, or
- active psychosis.

Play 2. Understand All the Rules

It is difficult enough to endure all of the big changes that occur when you go to rehab, residential treatment, or otherwise. Suddenly, you are expected to follow a schedule that is foreign to you, engage in discussions and behaviors that feel scary and unnatural to have, and even face trauma that has been swallowed down deep for a lifetime. But it's even more difficult to surrender your free will and follow a set of strict rules that you didn't set. I've seen time and again people struggle with the rules, and while they claim they have read them and learned them, with certain ones, people either misinterpret them, look for loopholes, or use them as excuses as to why they can't go to rehab or need to be prematurely discharged AMA.

One of the biggest issues, if not the biggest, that arises is when the answer is "No" to the burning question:

"Can I bring my dog to treatment?"

For many folks seeking treatment, their dog is their last friend and remaining family member. Often treatment has been delayed or forfeited because a person with a substance use disorder couldn't find a dog sitter. And to be frank, not being able to leave your dog is a hell of an excuse *not* to go to treatment. Investing in your future, however, is the best thing that you can do for your dog.

I have seen service dogs work out beautifully in treatment. It's humbling to see these devoted animals lovingly doing their tasks to keep their person safe and healthy. I have also seen it go south when the dog misbehaves, has a bowel or bladder oops, or jumps on another resident's bed. All of these situations can be addressed by doing the research beforehand and having an open dialogue with the treatment program.

There are often misunderstandings over the difference between pets and working animals (both service and emotional support animals). Not understanding what the law requires regarding both is what causes confusion, resentment, and failure to seek or complete treatment.

Pets

Delaying treatment because you can't decide on long-term care for your pet is understandable, but it cannot be an excuse. Today, people in recovery have many options available for finding dog care while in rehab.

Most treatment facilities don't let people bring their pets. Believe it or not, having your pets around can be a distraction. Remember, the whole purpose of rehab is to focus on overcoming your addiction and getting healthier. Sometimes, to achieve this, you need to separate yourself from those you love, including your dog.

Working Animals (Service and Emotional Support)

According to the ADA, a service animal is fully trained to perform tasks that are directly related to one's disability, and must be under the control of its handler. I have seen effective use of a service animal in treatment for the visually impaired, seizure disorder and diabetes.

The ADA website page "ADA Requirements: Service Animals," covers some rules about service animals:

> "When it is not obvious [to a treatment program] what service an animal provides, only limited inquiries are allowed. Staff may ask two questions: (1) is the dog a service animal required because of a disability, and (2) what work or task has the dog been trained to perform.
>
> Staff cannot ask about the person's disability, require medical documentation, require a special identification card or training documentation for the dog, or ask that the dog demonstrate its ability to perform the work or task....
>
> A person with a disability cannot be asked to remove a service animal from the premises unless: (1) the dog is out of control and the handler does not take effective action to control it or (2) the dog is not housebroken."

Some programs will ask you to make alternate arrangements for the dog if things don't go well, so that the client stays in treatment.

It is a common misconception that the ADA protects emotional support animals. However, the ADA only states that a person can bring a trained service dog to any public place, with the public place having no right to turn the animal away. The ADA does not include emotional support animals or animals other than dogs, meaning a public place reserves the right to deny entry to an emotional support animal.

There are a handful of treatment centers that are considered "pet friendly" and will allow you to bring your pet regardless of its status as a service animal. They are usually pricey, self-pay options and require that the dog

- is current on vaccinations,
- is treated for fleas and ticks,
- is leash-trained,
- remains in the resident's room when not being walked or taking bathroom breaks, and
- not be aggressive in nature.

Play 3. Look Forward to Step-Downs, a.k.a. Graduation

Treatment completion is marked not just by the passage of time, but by the progress one makes on achieving treatment goals and receiving the blessing of your treatment team that you are ready to move on.

As we have discussed, insurance programs do impact this decision; however, clinicians are skilled at prepping you for the next level of care if they believe that your insurance company is going to step you down early. What's critical is that you have the blessing of your team to step down or leave care and that there has been progress on your goals. If you are not ready to step down, your treatment team can advocate on your behalf with your insurance company.

Programs recognize treatment completion in a number of ways, which can be executed beautifully and emotionally.

> *Coin outs*—group members and staff put a message on a coin (or other relic) or share their favorite memory of the group member and

offer them a physical token to commemorate their journey. Some centers will ask family members to attend. I've seen family members blown away after hearing strangers talk about the impact that their loved one has had on the community. Residents often play songs that remind them of their treatment, and the group sits quietly and listens. In my care, we often wrote notes of all the affirmations that were made and then provided them to the client for relapse prevention, as well as a recording of the songs.

Music messages—specifically "your song" and your groups' songs can be put in a playlist when you need to reconnect with your healing space and emotions. The words and music can be used to remind yourself that you are loved, this was real, and the treatment program was your sacred place of healing. This all becomes a part of relapse prevention. In early relapse, "treatment trashing" is an early warning sign. When we start to focus on "the food was bad" or "my counselor was mean" and focusing on the negative, we can lose sight of the magic that we witnessed. It was very effective for my clients to have the tangible tools of the affirmation and music to take them back to their safe space. One particularly brilliant alumni director had a twenty-four-by-seven camera overlooking the mountains near the program so that alumni could "check in" online with their sacred space.

Work It!

Every time I hear "Into the Mystic" or "Bless the Broken Road," I'm transported back to the coin out ceremonies, from many years ago, and still feel the love and hope that surrounds the patients who chose those songs.

What songs move you?

What is your theme song for this moment in time?

What is the soundtrack of your life as you think about where you are right now as you read this book?

If you wanted someone to know you through the music of important life events, which songs would be most apt?

Treatment completion is really a commencement—a beginning of the next stage of your recovery journey as you leave your treatment team and discover the life you deserve. It is not a mistake that graduation ceremonies are mostly rituals that arm graduates with practical, tangible tools, like coin outs, music, and affirmations, to take with them. Professionals have been there. Most of them are in recovery and are well aware that the name of the game after the finish line is preventing relapse and being equipped to handle relapse, *if* it becomes a part of your recovery process.

CHAPTER 12

TAKING ADVANTAGE OF TREATMENT CENTER RESOURCES

The Plays for Continued Sobriety

"Progress is not achieved by luck or accident, but by working on yourself daily."

—EPICTETUS

Many folks will agree that the first forty-eight hours after discharge from treatment are the most difficult. Leaving the safe haven where you felt understood and bonded to people who feel what you feel and know what you know can be scary. This precarious time is bittersweet because people get to see their loved ones again and resume their lives but are leaving trusted members of their group, who they found hope and strength in. The difficulty marked by this forty-eight-hour period is so well-known that a renowned treatment center,

Sierra Tucson, published a book to help prepare others for life after discharge.

Nothing Changed but Me: Real Recovery Stories 48 Hours After Leaving Treatment chronicles thirty-three people who embarked on the journey of recovery and change and discovered that the first forty-eight hours upon leaving treatment required the same strength and courage they had to muster when they made the decision to go to treatment. Part of the online description of the book's purpose reads:

> Everyone's experience might be different coming in, but one thing is the same going out: the fear, the uncertainty, the uncomfortable anticipation about a new life that they can live if they choose to keep the light burning inside that was lit during treatment.... Knowing they are not alone and hearing from people who have told their stories in their own words, in a very personal, open and honest way, is an eye-opener for anyone who has gone to residential treatment, or who has supported loved ones in recovery.

Ultimately, hearing firsthand accounts from treatment alumni, like the ones that comprise this book, is a powerful resource to add to your relapse prevention plan. Chapter 2 chapter, we discussed internal and external triggers, warning signs, and high-risk situations, here we will discover the different resources available to you to arm you against such things that might come your way. Make them your plays as you learn to sustain sobriety and recovery.

Play 1. Participate in Your Alumni Group

An important part of your relapse prevention planning process is connection with your program's alumni resources. Alumni are people who have completed the program. Some treatment programs have over ten thousand alumni, with thousands who regularly participate in events. That's a lot of sobriety—and a whole lot of hope. Stand on their shoulders and peek into the possibility of having the life you deserve. The inspirational alumni community shows the power of community, treatment, and those who came before you. You will immediately have a place to belong—even without the walls of your treatment center.

Most treatment programs will facilitate an introduction to the alumni team while you are still in treatment so that you know the players and understand the resources available. Some of the things that are offered by alumni programs are annual weekend retreats, groups, virtual events, jobs boards/referral programs, and holiday support. It's all there for you, and most often, at no charge.

I have met alumni who had been sober since the late 1980s. Some folks who were in treatment together meet every year at their annual alumni reunion. The stories of success and tragedies are important in the recovery process, as we celebrate those who won their battle against their disease and mourn those we lost. When we lose someone to the disease, we all lose.

Alumni play a critical role in supporting ongoing recovery. After completing treatment, individuals often face the challenge of maintaining their sobriety and integrating back into their daily lives. Alumni programs provide a vital support network that helps individuals stay connected to the recovery community. Through continued engagement, alumni receive ongoing encouragement, accountability, and resources that reinforce their commitment to recovery. The sense of belonging and shared experiences among alumni can significantly enhance long-term recovery outcomes.

For Fans and Family

If you are looking for a treatment program for a loved one, ask your admissions representative to connect you to two or three alumni, one who graduated within the last year or so and someone who has been in long-term recovery. In addition to staff, speaking to a few alumni will give you an impression of their treatment experience. It will also provide context into what recovery looks like and prepare you to help your loved one. Beware of making your decision solely based on online reviews. Typically, those platforms are utilized by a disgruntled patient or someone who is struggling with their own demons. Rarely are negative online reviews an accurate depiction of what goes on behind the walls. Many solid treatment programs are misrepresented by posts from angry former patients who are upset about not getting a refund that they thought they deserved.

If you are looking for your own treatment, speaking with alumni is well worth the time and effort.

Play 2. Explore the Resource of Recovery Coaching

The popularity of recovery coaching has exploded in the last decade. Recovery coaches are not therapists; they are usually in recovery themselves and are in the category of peer support.

There are many credible training programs that someone can complete to have the proper training and credentials to work in this role. Some treatment centers will offer recovery coaches as part of their alumni programs, while other programs will refer you to a known affiliate partner. Recovery coaches assist with the following:

- Accountability
- Mentoring
- Accompanying to appointments
- Connecting to recovery resources

Recovery coaches can be invaluable when it comes to support, motivation, attending events, and staying on track with goals. Most recovery coaches will oversee the toxicology screening process and use an agreed-upon protocol if there is a positive test result. Their handling of the toxicology relieves the loved ones from the stress of being the "drug tester" and makes their role feel less like the "enforcer" or "warden" and more of an emotional support system.

Many recovery coaches, as well as employers, use a screening tool called Soberlink. Soberlink is a handheld, portable device designed for alcohol monitoring. The device uses a breath sample (with facial recognition technology to verify identity) to detect the presence of alcohol. An immediate blood alcohol concentration reading is done and instantly transmitted to the designated parties. The process is discreet and court admissible.

I've heard too many stories of clients with court-ordered breathalyzers on their vehicle (meaning that they have to blow into a device to start their car) asking their children to do it for them, creating dangerous situations and trauma on so many levels.

The Recovery Coaching Application

To supplement a live support person, treatment centers use several apps to provide alumni support. From calendars, daily inspirational quotes, communication capability, and 12-step information, it really does seem the be true that "there's an app for that." I had the honor of working alongside a team that created an app based upon the fundamentals of our program. The thousands of lives that are still being impacted by the talented alumni team that we had trained as recovery coaches remains one of the highlights of my professional career.

For Fans and Family

The availability of the over-the-counter drug naloxone (with the brand name Narcan) has been a significant response to the opioid crisis to reverse known or possible opioid overdoses. Naloxone is a prepackaged one-dose nasal spray administered by spraying one spray in one nostril of an affected person. An affected person can be quickly restored to normal breathing if their breathing has slowed or stopped because of an overdose.

If you or a loved one uses opioids, it's wise to keep naloxone at home, at your office, or in your vehicle. Ask your family members to carry it with them as well, and let friends know where you keep it stored. It is important to know that in the event of an overdose, people should still call 911 immediately and stay with the affected person to receive medical attention, as the medication only works in the body for up to ninety minutes.

Naloxone is being used more frequently by police officers, EMTs, and non-emergency first responders. You will find naloxone on hand at most treatment centers and in therapists' offices.

As the GoodRx article "How to Get Free Narcan to Keep at Home" describes, "In 2023, Narcan [naloxone] nasal spray became available over the counter for less than $50. You can still

Circle of Support

In a previous position, our coaching platform included an app and live coaches and had been active for about a year with outstanding results. One day, the recovery coach supervisor came running into my office and said that we had an emergency. One of our enrollees, an alumna, had reached out to him via the app and said that he was alone and intoxicated on a boat in the middle of a lake. He had two bottles of sleeping pills and was going to end his life. He reached out to our coach and asked him to tell his daughter that he loved her.

The complication here was that he was out of the country, and we had no easy way to get ahold of a first responders/crisis team. Fortunately, another coach kept him on the line, so we knew where he was and were able to contact the authorities who could reach him via boat or helicopter.

We were also able to get a three-way call going with his daughter to remind him of how much he was loved and needed. We all stayed on the line until the authorities reached him by boat and brought him to a hospital where he would stay until his daughter arrived.

His daughter jumped on the first plane and brought him immediately back to our treatment center. Within forty-eight hours of his distress call to his recovery coach, he was safely tucked in with us. This story is an amazing testimony to alumni/recovery coaches and their connection and ability to build trust. The impact of our work and a million "what ifs" were playing in my head for days. Mostly, I was overcome with a profound sense of gratitude that we are able to do this work. This app and recovery coaching program are still going full force and saving lives.

get the nasal spray…at pharmacies with a prescription and may pay less than the [over-the-counter] price.… Free Narcan [naloxone] is available from clinics, through the mail, in vending machines, and at libraries." To order, you can use the National Harm Reduction Coalition's "Naloxone Finder" or Next Distro at www.naloxoneforall.org.

Play 3. Consider Recovery Housing

There are many housing options for you regardless of where you are in the treatment process. As we discussed in Chapter 3, Deciding Your Playing Field: The Plays for Choosing Appropriate and Effective Care, some partial hospitalization programs offer a boarding option as part of the program. There are often very safe environments with supervision and support, like what is offered in residential treatment. Meals are prepared, shopping is done for you, and all basic needs are met.

In other cases, however, when you are in partial hospitalization or outpatient services, there will be options that are called transitional livings, sober livings, or halfway houses. They come in at all price points, offering a variety of supportive services depending on what your needs are. Some will require that you be in an active outpatient program, others will be supportive if you have a job, a therapist, and are going to meetings. I have worked with some clients who stay in their sober living for over a year while they transition back to work.

Let's review sober housing options and see what they offer:

Sober Living

Sober living is just like it sounds, a place to stay where you'll have a supportive community and learn to live a life free of drugs and alcohol. When leaving residential treatment, or the bubble, being in Sober Living is like dipping your toe in the real world and being able to return in the event to a safe space that is free of temptation and hopefully triggers. There is a built-in recovery community, and oftentimes the house managers are newer in recovery themselves. It is not uncommon for Sober Living residents to attend meetings together, and even host in house meetings with their Recovery Community. Making a commitment to abstinence and continued treatment of some type is most often a requirement of Sober Living homes. If the Sober Living homes don't require ongoing treatment, full time employment or school is a requirement. I have worked with many clients who live in a Sober Living for a year or more while returning to school or work. Some residents may not have completed residential treatment and their point of entry for care is Outpatient (PHP or IOP) with Sober Living. Most sober-living homes will be fine with, or even encourage, medically assisted treatment or other medications, as long as you are under the care of a physician. Drug tests are also an important part of the accountability factor in a Sober Living, keeping all residents safe.

Many treatment programs will have their own sober-living accommodations, and the language, rules, and even staff are consistent with the residential program.

The Betty Ford Foundation page about looking for sober-living houses describes the four categories of sober-living environments, as defined by the National Alliance for Recovery Residences:

Level 1 Peer-Run: These are often single-family homes that are democratically run, typically with a senior resident holding other residents accountable. Drug screenings and house meetings are typical, but there are no paid clinical positions within the home.

Level 2 Monitored: These are typically single-family homes or apartments. They can be run by a senior resident or a house manager with at least one compensated position. Drug screenings and house meetings are typical as well as peer-run groups and house rules.

Level 3 Supervised: This type of dwelling varies, but the facility is typically licensed and there is organizational hierarchy, administrative oversight, policies, and procedures. Life skills development is emphasized, and clinical services are provided outside of sober-living services. Staff are certified, and drug screenings are standard. [Level 3 is most often associated with a treatment center.]

Level 4 Integrated: Services tend to be provided in a more institutional environment and are often transitional services for those completing an addiction treatment program. Clinical services are provided in-house with a strong emphasis on life skills development. Staff are credentialed and drug screening is standard. [Level 4 is most often offered by a partial hospitalization program.]

In some sober-living homes, if you relapse, you may be asked to leave the home for up to seventy-two hours for the safety of the other residents. Another program might be arranged for you to attend briefly before returning or a higher level of care might be recommended.

Halfway House

Halfway houses are very similar to other sober-living residences, and the term is often incorrectly used interchangeably. The term "halfway house" comes from the idea that they serve as the halfway point between an institution and independent society. Some of the clients may be court-mandated to be there and may be coming from a correctional facility.

The halfway houses I have worked with require their tenants to have employment and will assist in finding them day labor jobs, while actively seeking full-time work.

As you can see, sober-living environments vary widely and depend on a variety of factors including budget, location, and ownership. The number of residents depends on the size of the home or licensed beds in a facility. In most sober-living environments, bedrooms are shared, to reinforce the sense of community, but some, especially the higher end, do offer the option for a private room. Each facility may be structured differently in terms of rules including maintenance and chores, visitor hours, mealtimes, curfews, and 12-Step meeting requirements.

The Betty Ford Foundation article also covers your potential length of stay in a sober-living facility:

> "The time spent in a sober-living home depends on a number of factors including strength of

> recovery from addiction, progress on clinical milestones, and the personal living situation at home. A minimum stay of three months is often recommended, but many [people] benefit from [both a shorter and] a longer stay."

Sober livings on the beach or in ski destinations are more expensive than those in more modest settings. When you're looking for a sober-living home, that you understand what is included in the monthly feed and what services are ala-carte. Don't make any assumptions and be stuck with a large bill at the end of your stay.

Examples of services offered in sober living that can cost extra include transportation to appointments, recovery coaching, extra meals, and gym memberships. Sober livings are not hotels, and being self-sufficient in terms of the tasks of daily living may be healthy steps to take. It may have been a while since you did laundry or cooked a meal, and it may be fun. Most sober-living owners have the right intentions and will work with you on pricing and payment plans. I've seen owners trade out part of the rent for yard work. Don't be afraid to ask what accommodations/barter arrangements can be made.

Finding a sober-living home can be a complicated process. If you are completing treatment, your program will either have their own program or recommend a vetted partner. If you are searching on your own be sure to not only take a tour of the facility, ask to speak with managers, current and former residents, and a professional affiliated with the sober living to determine if this place is the right choice for your recovery.

Play 4. Assess Your Recovery Capital

Over the past decades, treatment programs and insurance payers have understood the need for outcome data to determine what is the most effective mode of treatment delivery. We, as treatment providers, also look at things beyond sober or not sober. We like to know how the quality of life has improved and how you are doing in other domains of life such as job, relationships, health, and so on.

As treatment providers, we measure ourselves and our own success in treatment delivery, as well as compare our results against other providers. You may be asked to participate in what we call measurement-based care throughout the natural course of treatment. Most centers will screen your depression and anxiety at the onset of treatment, midway, and upon discharge. This provides all of us with a great report card of your progress and our effectiveness during treatment.

Your alumni team or coaches will also check in with you at various intervals post discharge, usually at six and twelve months. Please respond to their questions openly and honestly, not only to assess your progress, but to give back to the treatment community. Help us help the next person who comes through our doors in the most effective way possible. This means assessing each aspect of your life and sharing how recovery has impacted your overall mental and physical health, home life, cultural and social communities, and so much more. These things are the capital that make up your recovery life.

"Recovery capital" refers to the internal and external resources you can draw upon to support your recovery. Just like in a monetary portfolio, the idea is to build capital in your recovery. The more recovery capital, the wealthier you are in supporting yourself in your journey. Every day is an opportunity to acquire a new asset, strengthen the capital you have, or set new goals to achieve new assets.

"Recovery Capital is the breadth and depth of internal and external resources that can be drawn from to initiate and sustain recovery from alcohol, substance and other addictive behavior problems."
—White, W. & Cloud, W. (2008). Recovery capital: A primer for addictions professionals. Counselor, 9(5), 22-27.
Recovery Capital: A Primer for Addictions Professionals
William L. White, MA and William Cloud, PhD

The R1 Learning blog post about recovery capital describes the Substance Abuse and Mental Health Services Administration's four main areas to support a life:

1. **Health**, defined as overcoming or managing one's disease(s) or symptoms by making informed, healthy choices that support physical and emotional well-being
2. **Home**, defined as having a safe and stable place to live
3. **Purpose**, defined conduct[ing] meaningful daily activities such as a job, school volunteerism, family care taking or creative endeavors. Having the independence, income, and resources to participate in society
4. **Community**, having relationships and social networks that provide support, friendship, love, and hope

Recovery capital provides the roadmap for sustained recovery that goes beyond treatment and therapeutic interventions.

Without recovery capital, the most successful treatment episode in the world may not result in sustained recovery.

A higher level of recovery capital is generally associated with better outcomes, including sustained sobriety, better quality of life, and lower risk of relapse. It is an ongoing process to build recovery capital. Doing so requires effort, self-reflection, and the support of others.

Measuring one's recovery capital is done through the Assessment of Recovery Capital that was created in a 2012 paper by Teodora Groshkova, David Best, and William White. It is a tool that collects information on each major dimension of recovery capital. The tool provides clinicians and patients alike with essential information to be used as a centerpiece of care planning discussion at the clinical, recovery-coach, or peer-support levels. In the next section, you will learn to take the assessment for yourself and use it as a baseline and check-in to support and evolve your recovery goals.

Work It!

What is my recovery capital?

Complete the following assessment and follow the instructions for scoring.

Tick the statements that you agree with.

1. Having a sense of purpose in life is important to my recovery journey
2. I am able to concentrate when I need to
3. I am actively involved in leisure and sport activities
4. I am coping with the stresses in my life

5. I am currently completely sober
6. I am free from worries about money
7. I am actively engaged in efforts to improve myself (e.g., training, education, and/or self-awareness)
8. I am happy dealing with a range of professional people
9. I am happy with my personal life
10. I am making good progress on my recovery journey
11. I am proud of my home
12. I am proud of the community I live in and feel a part of it
13. I am satisfied with my involvement with my family
14. I cope well with everyday tasks
15. I do not let other people down
16. I am free of threat or harm when I am at home
17. I am happy with my appearance
18. I engage in activities and events that support my recovery
19. I eat regularly and have a balanced diet
20. I engage in activities that I find enjoyable and fulfilling
21. I feel physically well enough to work
22. I feel safe and protected where I live
23. I feel that I am in control of my substance use
24. I feel that I am free to shape my own destiny
25. I get lots of support from friends
26. I get the emotional help and support I need from my family

27. I have a special person that I can share my joys and sorrows with
28. I have access to opportunities for career development (job opportunities, volunteering, apprenticeships)
29. I have enough energy to complete the tasks I set
30. I have had no "near things" about relapsing
31. I have had no recent periods of substance intoxication
32. I have no problems getting around [Do I have transportation issues?]
33. I have the personal resources I need to make decisions about my future
34. I have the privacy I need
35. I look after my health and well-being
36. I make sure I do nothing that hurts or damages other people
37. I meet all my obligations promptly
38. I regard my life as challenging and fulfilling without the needs for using drugs or alcohol
39. I sleep well most nights
40. I take full responsibility for my actions
41. It is important for me to be involved in activities that contribute to my community
42. In general, I am satisfied with my life
43. It is important for me to do what I can to help other people
44. It is important to me that I make a contribution to society
45. My living space has helped drive my recovery journey

46. My personal identity does not revolve around drug use or drinking
47. There are more important things to me in life than using substances
48. What happens to me in the future mostly depends on me
49. I have a network of people I can rely on to support my recovery
50. When I think of the future, I feel optimistic

Scoring Instructions. For each statement marked, give yourself one point. The overall score is calculated by totaling all points, with higher Assessment of Recovery Capital scores indicating higher recovery capital.

When you review your scores, think about the following:

1. Am I surprised by anything? (positively or negatively)
2. Is there anything I want to improve upon immediately?
3. What two people can I share these results with?

Circle back in a few months and see if there are any changes, and then ask yourself questions one to three above.

Source: Teodora Groshkova et al. "The Assessment of Recovery Capital: Properties and psychometrics of a measure of addiction recovery strengths." ***Drug and Alcohol Review*** **32, no. 2 (2012): 187–194.**

As your recovery capital grows, you will experience growth and transformation in your life and in the lives of those you love. By executing the plays in *The Rehab Playbook*, although covered with blood, sweat, and tears, you will find that the win is living a life in recovery. That is the playbook's blessing. The support gained from your support group community, relieved loved ones, your team, and the treatment program alumni creates the tribe. At the center of the tribe is you.

You finally like yourself even when the pink cloud lifts and we have our series of firsts: first sober sex, sober holidays, sober work functions, sober business trips, and sober weddings. With your tribe around you, and a lot of prayer and meditation, you make it through. Then you show others the way and become part of their tribe. It's a beautiful thing. These series of firsts are replaced by the legacy of recovery, hope, and healing for you and your loved ones.

Recovery and healing, like so many things, are not linear. Some days will be better than others—and that's okay. Please tuck this book away and pull it out if you feel that you need a refresher on a topic, or if you want to pass it along to a friend or loved one. Be gentle and compassionate with yourself as you move through your beautiful life. God bless.

EPILOGUE

RECOVERY AS A PROFESSIONAL CALLING

Thank you for putting in the heartfelt effort of working through the steps and plays of *The Rehab Playbook*. Congratulations. Whether it is for you or a loved one, time spent in the pursuit of recovery is never a bad idea, as it can and will create miracles. Many folks who struggled with addiction are out there living lives full of peace and purpose.

Part of the joy of recovery is helping others, and there is always room for another to join on the recovery journey. Through the pages of this book, I pray that the message is clear: you are not alone. In fact, if you are ever in an airport, mall, or even casino and you feel like you need support, just ask someone to announce that "a friend of Bill W." needs assistance. Someone will come running.

If you are intrigued by the stories in our "team meetings," tremendous opportunity lies ahead. In the treatment industry, we are plagued by staffing shortages at every level. A therapist can now make double what they made in 2014 by joining a virtual platform, and many are choosing to practice out of their home and make more money, rather than working in a treatment center. Techs can take a job at In-N-Out Burger or Amazon and make more than they can in a treatment center. Why can't we just pay our staff more? Unfortunately, reimbursements from insurance companies have not risen with inflation to cover the costs of staff, food, insurance, housing, medications, and necessary labs. This makes the return on investment difficult for the owners of treatment centers. Whether the centers are privately owned, private equity–owned, or part of a publicly traded company, they are feeling the squeeze. We have an ethical obligation to run sustainable enterprises providing ethical quality care, whether the program is a $100,000 per month privately paid luxury program or a state-funded Medicaid program.

In many cases, the challenge of finding quality staff is what prevents us from getting help to the people who need it. After reading the stories shared in this book, my hope is you are inspired to join the profession. In no other profession can you have such an immediate impact on others, and they on you. The potential career trajectory for team members is unlimited. One can advance from tech to admissions director, tech to CEO/president, therapist to CEO, or patient to founder. This growth is divinely inspired and proportional to your effort, skills, fortitude, compassion, and ability to collaborate with others. The stories and contributions of the individuals who were in the "team meetings" can be your legacy as well, as you make your own contributions. Perhaps it is in the field of behavioral health where you will fulfill your purpose and be remembered for years to come.

We get more than we give to our clients. If we allow it, our clients will teach us all we need to know about ourselves.

They show us why everything matters. Where else can you go in your professional life to uncover your purpose and become exactly who you were meant to be? Or become a better version of yourself?

It was a blistering summer day in Arizona, and I was with two of my kids who were middle-school aged. A lovely young woman walked up to us and said, “Jaime, you probably don’t remember me.” As if I could ever forget her. She looked at my son, Joey, and said, “Kid, your mom saved my life. How cool is that?”

He smiled and said, “I’m really glad you are okay, but honestly, I’ve heard that about her a lot.”

In that moment, I knew that if my life ended tomorrow, it was a life well-lived.

GLOSSARY OF TERMS

The terminology and concepts in *The Rehab Playbook* are widely used in the addiction treatment world. Following is a recap of frequently used phrases, slang, and acronyms, followed by a brief definition. This list is by no means intended to be exhaustive.

Addiction: According to the American Society of Addiction Medicine, addiction is a treatable, chronic medical disease. It involves complex interactions among brain circuits, genetics, the environment, and an individual's life experiences.

AA: Alcoholics Anonymous is an international, abstinence-based support group rooted in the fellowship of individuals with alcohol use disorder.

Alcoholic: A stigmatizing term used to describe a person with alcohol use disorder.

AOD: Alcohol and Drugs.

AODA: Alcohol and other drug abuse.

Big book: One of the more popular addiction recovery terms used to describe the book *Alcoholics Anonymous,* also referred to as the "basic text." The foundational book of the AA program outlines the 12 steps, and 12 traditions, and includes personal stories of recovery.

BAC: Blood Alcohol Content is the percentage of alcohol units in someone's bloodstream.

Binge Drinking: For men, drinking 5 or more standard alcoholic drinks, and for women, 4 or more standard alcoholic drinks on the same occasion on at least 1 day in the past 30 days.

Buprenorphine: Also known as Subutex, is an opioid used to treat opioid use disorder, acute pain and chronic pain.

Clean: A stigmatizing term used to describe a person who has ceased substance use, having previously been addicted.

Clean time: A term used to describe the amount of time a person has been continually abstinent from substances. "Clean time" is celebrated in 12 Step fellowships such as CA and NA.

Closed meetings: AA meetings that are only open to members, or those who desire to quit their alcohol use.

CNS: Central nervous system refers to the nerve tissues that control the activities of the body, comprised of brain and spinal cord.

Cold Turkey: One of the addiction recovery slang terms used to describe the abrupt and complete cessation of taking a drugs.

Comorbidity: Two disorders or illnesses within the same person. Also referred to as dual diagnosis or co-occurring disorders.

Compulsion: A strong, usually irresistible impulse to perform an act. This can often be an act that is irrational or contrary to one's will.

Coping strategies: Efforts used to manage stressful events and difficult thoughts and emotions. Often referred to healthy or unhealthy (maladaptive).

Crack: Crack is the solid form of cocaine and is therefore administered either intravenously or by smoking from a crack pipe. Crack is stronger and more addictive than cocaine as it is condensed.

Craving: A powerful desire or urge to use a substance.

Clean: One of the stigmatizing addiction recovery terms used to describe an individual who is sober.

DOC: Drug of choice.

Doctor Shopping: Seeing multiple doctors in order to obtain multiple prescriptions.

Downers: A slang term for depressants and sedatives. Substances that depress the brain and CNS.

Dry Drunk: A term used to describe a person who has gone dry and stopped drinking but has not changed anything else in terms of behavior or their life.

DUI: Driving under the influence.

DWI: Driving while intoxicated.

Euphoric recall: When a person affected by a substance use disorder recalls the "good times" associated with substance use and subconsciously negates to recall of the consequences.

Fidelity: The extent to which an intervention is delivered as it was designed and intended to be delivered.

Functioning alcoholic: One of the addiction recovery slang terms used to describe a person who suffers from alcohol addiction but can function occupationally.

Harm Reduction: Strategies aimed at reducing substance use as well as negative consequences associated with substance use.

LOS: Length of stay pertains to the number of days, weeks, or months that a client remains in residential treatment, typically 30 to 60 days.

MAT: Medication-assisted treatment involves the use of medications in combination with other therapies.

Methadone: A synthetically produced, long-acting opiate used to reduce withdrawal. It is often used as a medication for helping stabilize and facilitate recovery.

Naloxone: A synthetic drug, similar to morphine, which blocks opiate receptors in the nervous system. It can reverse overdose from opioids. Sold commonly under the brand name Narcan.

Naltrexone: A medication primarily used to manage alcohol or opioid use disorder by reducing cravings and blocking the action of opiates.

Narcan: A medication used to reverse overdose from opioids. Naloxone.

Open meetings: Meetings open to individuals outside of AA, including those who do not have alcohol use disorder. Meetings are open to family members, loved ones, and general observers.

Peer support groups: Non-clinical groups in which individuals participate in conversations and activities that engage, educate, and support those struggling with and recovering from addiction.

Pink cloud: A stage in early recovery from addiction. This state involves feelings of excitement, confidence about recovery, euphoria, and elation.

PAWS: Post-Acute Withdrawal Syndrome refers to the set of symptoms that can persist for weeks or months after abstaining from a substance of abuse

Straight-Edge: One of the addiction recovery slang terms used to describe those who refrain from drugs, alcohol, tobacco, and sex.

Suboxone: A prescription medication used to treat opioid addiction that is a combination of buprenorphine and naloxone.

SI: Suicidal Ideation refers to having suicidal thoughts, thinking about and imagining suicide.

Tolerance: The physical effect of repeated use of a substance when it loses its effect over time.

Toxicity: A diverse array of adverse effects which are brought about through drug use at either therapeutic or non-therapeutic doses.

White Knuckling: A term used to describe a person who is struggling to maintain their recovery without outside support.

Sources: Substance Abuse and Mental Health Services Administration (US); Office of the Surgeon General (US). Facing Addiction in America: The Surgeon General's Report on Alcohol, Drugs, and Health [Internet]. Washington (DC): US Department of Health and Human Services; 2016 Nov.

Other Resources and Websites

Adult Children of Alcoholics & Dysfunctional Families (ACA)

www.adultchildren.org

American Social of Addiction Medicine (ASAM)

www.asam.org

SAMSHA (Substance Abuse and Mental Health Services Administration)

www.samsha.org

FindTreatment.gov is a product of SAMHSA's Center for Behavioral Health Statistics and Quality (CBHSQ). FindTreatment.gov provides the ability to search for substance use and mental health facilities, health care centers, buprenorphine practitioners, and opioid treatment providers.

www.findtreatment.gov

National Institute on Drug Abuse

www.nida.nih.gov

988 Lifeline

988 Lifeline offers free and confidential support for anyone in crisis. That includes people who need support for suicide, mental health and/or substance use crisis, or who are in emotional distress

ACKNOWLEDGMENTS

Thank you to all my colleagues and friends that were interviewed as part of this project. Your contribution to our field and the care that you provide for your patients is humbling. It is my honor to work with you all.

Thank you to Bobby Ferguson, Nick Kardaras, and Tena Moyer, your insights and stories are inspiring. I'm grateful to each of you.

Thank you to Sean Walsh, Jim Dredge, Jay Campbell, Joe Tinervin, Greg Kazarian, Maryann Rosenthal, Phil Herschman, Josh and Lisa Lannon, and Marvin Ventrell for believing in me along the way.

Thank you to Journey Healing Centers, Sierra Tucson, and Recovery Ways. I'm honored to have worked in each one of these sacred spaces alongside amazing teams.

Thank you to the Meadows Behavioral Health team for the honor of being your president. I am truly humbled to be a part of the MBH family.

Thank you to Michele Matrisciani for your partnership, guidance, and grace. This book would not be even close to what it is without you.

Thank you to Adam Chromy for your vision and encouragement.

Thank you to my husband Bill for your endless support, humor, and love.

ABOUT THE AUTHOR

Jaime Vinck, MC, LPC, NCC is the President of Meadows Behavioral Healthcare where she provides leadership and oversees the operations of both residential and outpatient programs. Jaime was previously the CEO of CPF Recovery Ways and the CEO of The Sierra Tucson Group. In 2019, she was named one of Arizona's Most Influential Women by *AZ Business Magazine*. Jaime has regularly been named one of the top leaders in *AZ* in both Healthcare and Behavioral Health, and is a mentor to women in leadership positions within the industry. Jaime serves as Vice Chair on the Executive Committee of the Board of Directors of the National Association of Addiction Treatment Providers.

Jaime speaks nationally and internationally on trending topics, including suicide, addiction and depression, compassion fatigue, and the importance of collaboration when treating co-occurring disorders. Jaime holds a bachelor's degree in labor and employee relations from Michigan State University and a master's degree in professional counseling from Ottawa University. She and her husband, Bill, live in Scottsdale, Arizona with their children and grandchildren.